County Council

Libraries, books and more . . .

1 7 APR 2015   WITHDRAWN

Please return/renew this item by the last due date.
Library items may be renewed by phone on
030 33 33 1234 (24 hours) or via our website
www.cumbria.gov.uk/libraries

Cumbria Libraries
CLIC
Interactive Catalogue

Ask for a CLIC password

D1349957

TEMPORARY
HEROES

LIEUTENANT NORMAN CECIL DOWN

RICHARD VAN EMDEN

Pen & Sword
MILITARY

To the only "Phyllis"

First published in Great Britain in 1917 by The Bodley Head

Republished in this format in 2014 by
PEN & SWORD MILITARY
An imprint of
Pen & Sword Books Ltd
47 Church Street
Barnsley, South Yorkshire
S70 2AS

ISBN 978 1 78159 196 3

A CIP catalogue record for this book
is available from the British Library

Printed and bound in England
By CPI Group (UK) Ltd, Croydon, CR0 4YY

Pen & Sword Books Ltd incorporates the Imprints of Aviation, Atlas,
Family History, Fiction, Maritime, Military, Discovery, Politics, History,
Archaeology, Select, Wharncliffe Local History, Wharncliffe True Crime,
Military Classics, Wharncliffe Transport, Leo Cooper, The Praetorian Press,
Remember When, Seaforth Publishing and Frontline Publishing

For a complete list of Pen & Sword titles please contact
PEN & SWORD BOOKS LIMITED
47 Church Street, Barnsley, South Yorkshire, S70 2AS, England
E-mail: enquiries@pen-and-sword.co.uk
Website: www.pen-and-sword.co.uk

INTRODUCTION BY RICHARD VAN EMDEN

It is popularly assumed that life in the trenches was a long-drawn-out, miserable saga: unspeakable squalor was the norm, in which men were harried by incompetent generals, run over by rats, infested by lice, and lived knee deep in mud, their lives punctuated by regular bouts of terror and going over the top. The idea that humour had much part to play is near-heresy: the misery of trench life, it is held, guaranteed that there was not much to laugh about and every reason to be morose. In fact, humour was a life-saver, an integral part of service life, its regular expression keeping many men from mental collapse. It is a natural daily humour, often black in character, that under-pins this, one of the outstanding but forgotten books of the Great War. It was published in 1917 as a series of letters from a young officer, 'Thomas', to his fiancée, 'Phyllis'. In fact, the use of these names is the only fictitious element to the book; otherwise the letters are reproduced 'practically untouched', as the author, real name Cecil Down, says of his writing to Edith, the real name of his fiancée.

These letters are important. They are written by a man who possessed not only a special literary gift but also the perseverance to write on a very regular and frequent basis, so that they provide an unfettered snapshot of one soldier's war as it happened. Composed over an eighteen-month period from February 1915 until late July 1916, averaging almost one letter a week, they were written with no thought as to their future publication; it is not known whether or not he even asked Edith to hold on to the letters. The result is a story not reflected upon after the war, nor tampered with by reassessment or altered sentiment. 'They are impressions of the moment, and are subject to the fits of depression and optimism that attacked everybody in the trenches,' he asserted. There are other books of letters, of course, but few, very few, can write as well as Down did; indeed, his distinctive style is a rare gift.

Down's introduction appears modest, even slightly downbeat. 'This is no thrilling tale of daring-do,' he wrote, 'but a collection of letters written from all kind of places, mostly unpleasant, in all weathers, chiefly rain, and at all sorts of odd times.' Yet what he could not say is that they are beautifully written, vibrant and hugely entertaining.

Constitutionally, he is upbeat in outlook; his writing is not indicative of forced cheerfulness in order to safeguard the feelings of Edith, nor are the letters wildly optimistic for fear of appearing to be unpatriotic. There's no stiff-upper-lip here, but there are nevertheless tangible mood swings, permitting the reader to appreciate the nuances of the author's personality as one might understand in a good friend or close relative. Importantly, we appreciate that a soldier's stated opinion is not necessarily his view set in concrete, but often an immediate and transitory response to events often trivial and even banal. As Down points out, if he asserts that the war might be lost, this may be purely a reaction to the late arrival of the rum ration in the morning when thwarted expectations turn to sullen resentment.

Down writes eloquently of the army's politics. He describes cogently the arrangement by which orders are passed down the chain of command, and how ultimately the man who is praised for the successful completion of a back-breaking job is not, as a rule, the man who has physically undertaken the task, but the one charged with overseeing its implementation. He talks, too, of 'rest' from the front line, which was frequently not rest at all, but an opportunity to keep men on their toes through the necessary but, as he explains, the needlessly aggressive cleaning of equipment, physical exercise, practised skirmishing and endless route marches – deemed worthwhile, he claims, owing to the perceived inaction of life in confined trenches. Down is not overtly critical of these decisions, but rather prefers to cast his eye wryly over such rules and regulations, gently mocking their over-zealous interpretation but not their validity nor importance.

Grousing at such rules and regulations was as normal a state of affairs as making light of trying situations. Moans about conditions and daily demands made upon men in the line were directed, as Down says, at the much-maligned army staff. Complaining about the perceived failure or exaggerated demands of superiors gave vent and focus to petty frustrations; it bound men together in the trenches and out on rest, dissipating the inevitable aggression in an all-male environment and directing it at outside nebulous forces.

One of Down's greatest assets is the gift of mimicry. He listened to and captured conversations, the intonation and accents of other ranks and fellow officers, like no other author. He describes incidents with a panache that is not only delightful but surprisingly modern in delivery: his description of a court martial in which a man is accused of shooting a farmer's chickens, rings wincingly true of the sometimes amateurish way in which such courts could be conducted, and is so funny that it makes one laugh out loud.

On another occasion, he recalls an incident when, chewing a particularly large piece of toffee sent from home, he received a call from his irascible commanding officer.

'[I] tried to say hello but could not open my mouth,' he wrote. 'At the other end I could hear the CO cursing my lack of promptitude...the toffee had me in its grip.' In the end Down could offer nothing more than a long drawn out
'o-o-o-m.'
'That you?'
'o-o-o-m.'
'Why haven't you come before?'
'o-o-o-m.'
'You've been to sleep. You're half asleep now.'
'o-o-o-m.'
'You have, I can hear the sleepiness in your voice,' and thereupon he delivered me a lengthy lecture upon the subject of falling asleep at one's post, and the penalties involved, among them death...'

While the tone of the letters is buoyant, this did not mean that he shied away from describing incidents of pathos. Sometimes humour is the backdrop to what is clearly a poignant moment, but on other occasions he describes with disarming simplicity and accuracy moments of anguish; of a newly-formed mine crater he wrote:

'By the light of the moon you could see it all, the great yawning hole, a good fifty feet deep, with dead bodies stretched in ghastly attitudes down its steep sides. Every now and then one of the bodies, stirred by some explosion, would turn over and roll to the bottom, sliding down in a perfect shambles, where it would soon lose its identity among the jumbled heap of corpses and shattered limbs...'

Cecil Down was commissioned into the 4th Gordon Highlanders in September 1914. His battalion, a territorial unit, was sent to France as part of the 8th Brigade, 3rd Division, and his letters began two days after he stepped off the boat at Le Havre and with a typically forthright opening. His battalion served principally in the Ypres Salient throughout 1915, and he gives us vivid descriptions of the fighting and the destruction of the famous town just behind the line. He writes of the new gas masks issued to the troops after the first gas attack by the Germans in April and of the very heavy and prolonged shelling. He describes vividly, too, the strain and the difficulties of going over the top to secure limited but important objectives and of fighting near Sanctuary Wood in late September. In October, much to his evident relief, he was sent down the line to serve as a Bombing Officer to the 8th Brigade where he remained until well into the New Year.

In late February 1916, his battalion was transferred to the 51st Highland Division, and in April 1916, Cecil's new division moved down to the Somme where he rejoined his battalion. However, shortly afterwards he was sent on a month's course at the Infantry School from where he noted, while playing cricket, the opening salvos of the Somme Offensive. Soon afterwards, he once again rejoined his battalion, which had been undertaking a series of route marches behind the lines. At Bernaville, the battalion received orders to move towards the front, from where it marched through a concentrated and heavy bombardment to take part in an attack on High Wood, one of the most heavily defended German positions on the Somme. The Gordon Highlanders were to assault a newly-discovered trench system known as the Intermediate Line and a redoubt in the northeast corner of the wood, as part of a much larger attack on the entire German position.

'We are off into the thick of it this evening [21 July], up to that ill-fated wood half a mile in front of our line, so we shall see life with a vengeance...' Cecil wrote.

It would be six days before he was able to write again to let Edith know he was safe, though not entirely sound.

The attack was timed for 10pm on 23 July. Limitations on time ensured that no proper reconnaissance of the ground had been carried out before the Gordon Highlanders went over and into the wood. 'Our attack utterly failed,' wrote the adjutant in the battalion diary. The battalion lost over 60 men killed or died of wounds, including three officers, and a further nine officers and 190 other ranks were wounded, including Captain Cecil Down who was hit by shrapnel in the right thigh causing a long laceration. By 3am, the battalion was back in its original position.

Cecil was evacuated by Red Cross barge and as he approached the town of Abbeville he finally found the strength to write to 'Phyllis' to let her know that he was 'all right' and that 'my troubles are over now'. It is at this point that Cecil finishes his story with a flourish typical of the man. 'Your 'Thomas',' he concluded, 'what there is left of him'. From many other soldiers such a line might have sounded angry or bitter, but not from him.

Perhaps at Abbeville or later at a base hospital at Le Havre, Cecil was operated on and a piece of metal extracted from the top of his leg. A week later, he had left Le Havre for Southampton and the 3rd Southern General Hospital in Oxford, where he remained for a considerable time while the wound healed.

Released for convalescence, he was seen on a regular basis by a medical board that continued to mark him down as fit for Home Service only but not General Service. Perhaps bored from being under-employed, Cecil asked to be sent to the south east coast where he could undertake instructional duties; it would have also proved an opportune place for meeting his family, and also his fiancée who was in Sarre in Kent.

By the end of February, he was deemed fit once again. In the middle of November he was once again warned for overseas service. On 24 November, he was back in France.

On this occasion, Cecil's destination would not be the Western Front. Within a week he would be taken south by train to board a boat for the Mediterranean, to Palestine where he was attached to the 14th Black Watch, 229 Brigade, 74th Division. He would be in the Middle East for the next four months until, on 6 April 1918, at Abu Felah, he was slightly wounded in the head by a shell fragment, just days prior to the Division's complete removal from the front. He was evacuated to Egypt and a hospital in Cairo. 'I saw myself in a looking-glass, and nearly died of the painful process of laughing,' he wrote a few days after he was wounded. 'The whole of the right side of my face is enormous, like a gumboil, a thick ear, and a fat eye combined. Round the eye is all back and purple, and the white of the eye is red.' On 25 April he was operated on and a small piece of metal was removed as well as two pieces of stone that had been blasted into his head behind his right ear. The wound healed quickly.

Cecil Down's memoir of service in the Middle East was subsequently published and entitled *Temporary Crusaders*. It ends in mid-June 1918, shortly before he returned to France and the fighting around the Hindenburg line.

Norman Cecil Sommers Down was born on 9 September 1893 to James and Mary Down, at Satara in India, where his father was a police inspector. Returning to Britain, Cecil was educated at St Lawrence College, Ramsgate, and began work as a Civil Servant in 1912. In August 1917 he married 25 year old Edith Steddy and after leaving the army he settled down in Birchington-on-Sea, close to his wife's family in Kent. His first child had been born in 1918 (he was home on leave from France correcting the proofs to *Temporary Crusaders*, subsequently dedicating his efforts to his new-born daughter). A second daughter was born in 1921. Cecil eventually became a Senior Principal Inspector of Taxes, Board of Inland Revenue, and was honoured with a Companion, Order of St Michael & St George (CMG). Edith died in February 1961 aged just 68 and Cecil remarried a year later. He died 14 March 1984, aged 90.

FOREWORD

SOME talk of Alexander, and some of Hercules. And some don't. This is no thrilling tale of derring do, but a collection of letters written from all kinds of places, mostly unpleasant, in all weathers, chiefly rain, and at all sorts of odd times. They are the impressions of the moment, and are subject to the fits of depression and optimism which attack everybody in the trenches. Thus if in one letter serious doubts are entertained of our power to win it must be put down to the non-arrival of the rum issue, and if in another 'the war is said to be almost over that is a sign of the reopening of leave rather than any tangible evidence to that effect. The real actors have in every case given way to fictitious characters, but with this exception the letters are practically untouched. It may seem to some that the not infrequent references to the Staff do not show sufficient respect for that much maligned body, but it is necessary to remember that without something to grouse about life in the infantry would be unbearable, and the Staff forms a convenient target for the envenomed darts of the man whose billet leaks or who finds that his account is overdrawn. The writer would be the last to desire, as some people seem to do, an exchange of Staffs with the German Army.

7

CONTENTS

ILLUSTRATIONS

RUMOURS OF WARS

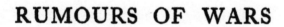

TEMPORARY HEROES

CHAPTER I

RUMOURS OF WARS

SOMEWHERE IN FRANCE,

February 22nd, 1915.

France is a fraud, Phyllis, France is a fraud
Here have we been led to believe for the last six
months that it is a land flowing with fair maidens,
free wine, and flower-strewn paths. And what do we
find ? First of all, horrible cobbly roads that hurt
your feet. You have to march on the wrong side of
them too. The roads, not your feet. The free wine is
in reality very bad beer, for which you have to pay
the fair maiden (generally about fifty years old) a
wholly exorbitant price. And they don't even seem to
understand their own language. At any rate they
could not " compree " my servant when he asked for
" twa bougies," which he assures me is correct French
for two candles. He knows this because a kind lady

presented him with a book of "Useful French Phrases" before we came out.

Our debut on foreign soil was marked by a pleasing incident. Our C.O. had never been in France before. Neither had the adjutant. So, when they saw a figure approaching them arrayed in gorgeous uniform, they jumped to the conclusion that it was some French general come to greet us. Accordingly we marched past him at attention, with eyes left, and the band playing "Hielan' Laddie." We found out afterwards that he was a private in the local *gendarmerie*. Still I expect he enjoyed the experience.

It was a brute of a march to the rest camp—five miles and all uphill. Poor little W., who prided himself on the completeness of his kit, began to have doubts about it after the first mile. At the end of the second he presented a small boy, who asked for "bulleebif," with his "bivouac, portable, one, officers, for the use of." Another mile saw him part with a Thermos flask, which he presented to a French soldier by the roadside. In the next mile a patent stove and a French dictionary went, and a spare electric light and two tins of chocolate rations also disappeared before the end of the journey. When we reached the camp we hoped to be allowed to throw off our packs and rest our aching limbs, but instead of that we were kept at attention for three-quarters of an hour, while some old gentleman had a look at us. S'pose that's why they call it a rest camp.

That was on the evening of the twentieth. The next

morning was spent in dishing out fur-coats. Mine is
rather quiet, black fox with musquash sleeves, or
thereabouts, but some of them are the very latest mode.
Lance-corporal McGregor, for instance, looks very
smart in his leopard skin with collar of skunk and cuffs
of polar bear. He is a fish porter by trade. The C.O.'s
is rather a nice little thing in Persian lamb, touches of
domestic cat about the yoke giving it a very chic
appearance.

In the afternoon some of us went down into the
town, which, by the way, is Le Havre—the men insist
on pronouncing the " Le " to rhyme with tea, but it's
a dull place for all that. When we got back there was
a pile of letters for each of us to censor. It was our
first experience and we were very thorough for a time,
but once the novelty wore off it became boring. None
of my platoon will ever be literary genii I fear. We
censor our own letters as well as those of our platoon,
but at first it was rumoured that one officer had to be
chosen to do those of all the others. This created
some heart-burning as all of us, barring the married
ones, had at least one letter not meant for the eyes of
any brother officer.

They say that we are off for the front to-morrow,
but you never know. Several of my men put in their
letters that they could hear the distant thunder of the
guns, but as we are about a hundred miles from any
fighting they must have keen ears.

The tent is becoming very cold, so I am going to
turn in.

As my servant writes, " I should like to send some xxxxs but the censor might laugh." Poor censor.

Good night.

Your

THOMAS.

MUDDY VIEW VILLA,

FLANDERS,

March 4th.

DEAR PHIL,

Muddy View Villa is a leaky wooden hut completely surrounded by moist Europe, ankle deep. It has a door which also serves as window, but most of the light comes through the cracks in the walls. Several hundred draughts swirl round and round inside, filling your throat with foul smoke from a brazier. A brazier, by the way, is a tin can with holes in it. It contains coke, which gives forth smoke and gas but no heat. In one corner of the hut there is an ornamental lake several inches deep. The other three corners are occupied by eight of us. This is a great life.

We left Havre on the day after my last epistle. The manner of our going was thuswise. We left the camp at 2 a.m. and marched down to the station (goods department). The station was deserted save for one voluble porter who declared (quite truthfully) that our train was to start about noon. Dawn as seen from

Havre Station on a frosty February morning is disappointing. About 6 a.m. a coffee stall opened. It was run by four English girls and proved a great blessing. Without it we should most certainly have turned to pillars of ice. As it was, my platoon sergeant's balaclava helmet froze on to his moustache, causing him pain when he tried to talk.

An hour or so later our train floated in and we were duly introduced. It consisted of over thirty cattle-trucks and one third-class carriage. The cattle-trucks bore the inscription :

CHEVAUX 8
HOMMES 33

but as we are only Territorials, forty men were bundled into each truck, together with a bale of hay. H.Q. and company commanders took possession of the third-class carriage and the rest of us shared a truck.

Half an hour before the train was due to start, it made up its mind to go, leaving about three hundred assorted officers, N.C.O.'s and men on the platform. We started after it on foot, running hard. It must have been quite a spectacle. Before it had gone half a mile most of us had caught up with it and boarded it. Then, again without warning, it stopped with a jerk, and didn't carry on till 2.30 in the afternoon.

Once it really got a move on, though, we kept up a pretty steady six miles an hour. Of course every time we came to a wayside *estaminet* the engine-driver descended for a glass of *vin blanc* and a chat, but we all realised that this was war at last and no one complained. As you have probably gathered, we were not on the main line. There had been a big smash somewhere, so we were sent a circular tour round a very hilly and altogether rural loop line. At each little station the villagers crowded round the trucks admiring our kilts and bare blue knees—the kilts I mean. There seemed to be no signals or controls of any sort on the line, and at one time no less than four trains could be seen behind us. Downhill steam was turned off and we ran along by the force of gravity at a great speed. We tore through one station on a down gradient at eighty miles an hour at least. This must have distressed the station-master who I am sure wanted to have a talk with the engine-driver. The station-master, by the way, was a woman.

As darkness came we closed the sliding doors, lit the lamps, and tried to get up a good frowst to last us the night. Despite the cold we fell off to sleep, but woke up with a jerk as the train came to a standstill. Outside it was dark and snow was falling. Someone out in the night shouted, " Calais." We turned in again and slept fitfully till dawn, at which hour we reached G.H.Q. From here onwards the journey became increasingly slow, and it was not till the afternoon that we reached X——, the railhead, a small town near the Belgian frontier.

Here we stayed for a day or two in glass-houses, the

largest in the world, so they say. Anyhow they were
very cold at night, and the floor was covered with
a sort of chaff which got into our eyes, ears, nostrils,
mouths, food, and everything. In the parts where
grapes are being grown the hot-water pipes are still
on. My servant discovered this, and a tub, and pro-
cured me a hot bath. Just as I was getting into it
along came a bevy of fair grape-pickers. Horrible
confusion. Moral—those who live in glass-houses
shouldn't have baths.

The chief amusement was to watch the traffic in the
square. Very early in the morning it is filled with
bedraggled groups of men plodding home from the
trenches, and with horse transport back from carrying
rations up to the firing line. Later comes the hour of
the supply column, when the little square vies with
Charing Cross. Unending streams of lorries pass and
repass, muddy and unkempt in their coat of dingy
grey, under which you can still make out the faint
outline of the peace-time owner's name. Allsopps',
Harrods', and many another firm's lorries jostle each
other here in just the same way as six months ago they
did in dear old London. A car flashes through full of
" red hats," and every now and then an ammunition
column trots by. A motor-bus pants along, its
windows boarded up and its grey coat all smeared with
mud. Only the notice-board on the top still proclaims
that once upon a time Camberwell Green was its
destination. Slowly and silently through it all glides
a convoy of motor-ambulances. You begin to feel

that there is a war on. All the houses in the main street are splattered with mud up to the windows of the second storeys.

Just as we were settling down to enjoy ourselves we were pushed off to join the brigade of regulars of which we are now members. The march was not long, but arduous for all that. While we were in France the roads were fairly good, but once the frontier was crossed and we were in Belgium they became too awful for words. For the most part Belgian roads are straight, and run through avenues of tall spiky trees, which resemble more than anything telegraph poles trying to pass themselves off as brussels sprouts. The middle of the road is made of small square stone blocks, and has a very abrupt *cambre*. This is called *pavé*, and is generally only just broad enough for one cart to pass along at a time. It is very slippery in wet weather. The sides of the roads are quagmires of reddish-brown mud, ankle-deep if you are lucky, and waist-deep if you aren't. When a lorry comes along you have to get off and wade through the slush. Ough——. Remember little Belgium! It's impossible to forget it when you've got about half of it clinging to your boots, and the other half splashed all over your person. At one place on the road there was a group of Belgians trying to bolster it up, under the guidance of an R.E. corporal. I think that Flemish must be the ugliest language in the world, a mixture of low German and bad French, with a liberal flavouring of billingsgate.

At last we arrived at our own particular slough of despond. It is just outside a little village, and some three miles from the trenches, and is a collection of wooden huts like the one I have already described. Oh, and there's an officers' mess too, but it hasn't got any door or glass in the windows, and only half a roof.

We've been messing round the last few days, learning to bomb and all that sort of thing. Bombing seems rather fun as the chances are even on the bomb exploding before instead of after leaving your hand. Each company is going into the trenches under the wing of one of the regular battalions. Our turn comes to-morrow, and we are busy preparing for it, so,

Au revoir.

Your

THOMAS.

P.S.—This place abounds in hop-poles. They are enormous, more like the masts of a ship. But though the Belgian hop-poles are very large, their beer is very small.

A Fire-trench,

March 14th.

Phyllis Mine,

Excuse the shakiness of my writing but the dug-out is trembling with suppressed emotion from the constant vibration of the Jack Johnsons, or so you might imagine to read some of my men's letters. The dug-out, by the way, is four foot long by two broad, and is full of draughts, mud, and other things, lots of—er, other things. And as I sit in it I am all that stands between the horrible Hun and you, on a front of five yards that is.

Since my last letter we have been in the trenches three times, first scattered among the men of a regular battalion, then as a platoon with a company of regulars, and now all on our own. On the first night going up I fell into a shell hole. There was much mud therein, and I issued forth a sadder and a wetter man. The worst of it was that I couldn't change a stitch for two days. This is a terrible war.

You ask how I felt under fire for the first time. Well, it was distinctly disappointing. It was at night, going up to the trenches. There was a funny sort of swish which I couldn't quite place, so I asked the guide what it was.

" Oo, nuffing much, sir, only a bullet."

Then I ducked. It wasn't very brave of me, was it ? Especially as the missile in question had long since gone to ground some hundreds of yards to the rear.

After a bit you begin to get accustomed to the sound, and get quite callous as long as you remember that, if the bullet really does hit you, you will be dead before you hear it. At least so the guide said. Of course, too, the bullets are not aimed at anyone special during the night, but just loosed off at intervals by an obedient sentry in the worthy endeavour to punish England. Shells aren't so nice. There is a sudden whizz—bang, or a sedate s-s-s-sh—w-h-u-m-p, as the case may be, and then you look at each other and laugh, if you're still there. Though what there is to laugh about beats me.

The people who showed us how the wheels go round were an English county battalion, composed chiefly of farm labourers. They were altogether topping to us. All Highlanders out here go by the name of Jocks, but these Tommies were inclined at first to refer to some of our more aristocratic privates as " young gentlemen."

One of them was a typical Tommy of the " 'Arf a Mo', Kaiser " type. I never found out his name but his friends called him Woodbine, and the company-sergeant-major referred to him as " that —— nuis-ance." He was a weedy-looking youth and had been out since Mons. A lock of raven hair struggled out from his cap-comforter, on the top of which his cap perched at an angle of forty-five to the vertical, peak over the left ear. His eyes were small but twinkled, and his mouth was simply great. In fact when he grinned it stretched from ear to ear. He was always singing—you could tell it was singing by the words—

and he was immensely dirty. Early one morning,
just as the German trenches were becoming visible,
he was found sitting on the parapet, chanting gloomily
to the tune of " Little Brown Jug " :

> " Ha ! Ha ! Ha ! He ! He ! He !
> Old fat Fritz, you can't see me."

But apparently he was wrong, for with a splutter
of earth a bullet plonked into a sandbag not a foot
from him. Undismayed he changed his dirge to :

> " Ha ! Ha ! Ha ! He ! He ! He !
> Poor old Huns, they can't hit me " ;

and continued until he was dragged down by his
sergeant amidst a storm of bullets. Such men are a
curse back in billets, but a heaven-sent blessing in
the trenches.

In billets you drill hard all day in case you forget that
you are soldiers. In support you eat and sleep all
day. By night you work jolly hard carrying rations
and material to the firing line, and digging more
trenches. For real peace give me the front line. Here
you eat and sleep by day; and by night you stand still
and wait for Fritz to attack. Similarly Fritz over the
way is waiting for you to do likewise, so you don't get
much forrader. The trenches just here aren't so very
wet—nowhere does the water come over your knees,
but that is because they aren't trenches at all, only
breastworks, built up of sandbags.

The farm in which we live when in support is of the

usual Belgian pattern—farm-house on one side of a square, barns on the other three, and a midden in the centre. A midden is a sort of pond into which the thrifty farmer throws his manure, and from which he draws his drinking water. Belgian water, by the way, is a light brown to look at, and hardly distinguishable either in colour or taste from their beer. My servant brought me some hot water to shave in this morning and I mistook it for soup. To get back to the support billet, we occupy the house and the men the barns. The barns never had any sides worth mentioning, and the house has lost most of its roof, so I don't know who is best off. Still I suppose we are, as we have a cellar. The cellar has rats. Also mice and frogs.

I shall have to stop now as it's " stand to " time.

Your gallant defender,

THOMAS.

THE PIGGERIES,

April 4th.

MY DEAR GIRL,

How can I thank you enough for the topping parcel, which arrived more or less intact last night. You are a dear to think of it. The only thing is that if I were you I shouldn't send any more corned beef. We get a pound of it every day as a present from Kitchener. It is generally known as bully beef, and, being a ration is despised by everybody. I'm afraid

that the average man hasn't yet grasped the idea that
the Government occasionally give us good stuff,
although it is possible to obtain bad. At any rate,
back in billets the men give away their biscuits and
bully and purchase very third-rate bread and doubtful
eggs instead. The only issue that is not looked down
upon is the nightly tot of rum and the tins of anti-
frostbite grease. I was nearly forgetting them. When
applied to the soles of the feet this grease will prevent
all sorts of things, or so the D.A.A.Q.M.G. (that's
correct to within a letter or two) would have us believe.
The men, however, resent any attempt to deprive them
of a nice little jaunt down the line with swollen feet,
and use it for purposes of " drumming up," which is
B.E.F. for cooking.

The toffee you sent was very good but a trifle sticky.
In fact its stickiness was almost my undoing. I was
on duty at 2 a.m. and to keep myself awake inserted a
large portion into my mouth. Almost at once a signaller appeared and told me that I was wanted on the
phone. I went to the signaller's abode, took up the
instrument, and tried to say " Hullo," but could not
open my mouth. My jaws were stuck tight. At the
other end I could hear the C.O. cursing my lack of
promptitude. Again and again I tried, but to no
purpose. The toffee had me in its grip. At last the
C.O. got wild and started to shout " Hullo " and other
less polite remarks down his end of the machine. This
time I managed to answer with a long drawn—

" O-o-o-m."

" That you ? "

" O-o-o-m."

" Why haven't you come before ? "

" O-o-o-m."

" You've been to sleep. You're half-asleep now."

" O-o-o-m."

" You have, I can hear the sleepiness in your voice," and thereupon he delivered me a lengthy lecture upon the subject of falling asleep at one's post, and the penalties involved, amongst them DEATH. All I could reply to his diatribe was " O-o-o-m," and it was not till morning that the matter could be satisfactorily explained.

I have never lived in a nicer pigsty. It has a stone floor and an arched roof of brick, and is divided into partitions. In one we eat, in another the O.C. Company sleeps noisily with the second in command, in the third the rest of us sleep and keep each other warm, and the fourth is inhabited by the few remaining swine. How ennobling is war, is it not ?

You say that rumour is as rife as ever over in England. Well, we don't escape from it here. Every day we hear that Italy has joined in, in fact that little story has become so common that the sigs. end up all their messages with " Italy has declared war " instead of the more official ac, ac, ac. Every week the German fleet is destroyed, and when nothing else is doing America generally declares war, first against one side and then against the other. Only yesterday two million of K.'s army and Winston Churchill landed at Ostend. So you see that it is no use your writing to tell me what is really happening.

Now I must go and inspect rifles. We keep them quite spotless these days lest the Hun catch us unawares, and, like the foolish virgins, we find ourselves in the soup.

Cheero.

THOMAS.

THE HUTS,

April 10th.

PHYLLIS MINE,

Back in billets again and very busy doing nothing in particular. It is surprising what a lot there is to do and how very little there is to show for it. The morning after our return from the trenches the men write letters to all the people they have ever known or are likely to know. About midday your sergeant puts his head through the door of your hut and hands you a hundred or so to carry on with. They are a ragtime collection.

The first one you open will probably be one of the " young hero " type and will contain some reference (untrue) to the constant thunder of the guns. The writer you gather is the only one of his section not suffering from " wind up," which is not surprising considering the awful time we are all having. The food is awful and totally insufficient, only a pound of bully beef and several handfuls of biscuit per day, not to mention tea, sugar, vegetables, and soup. Some men are never happy unless they are grousing.

Then comes the son anxious not to let his mother get an inkling that he is near the front. Either he gives lengthy descriptions of the surrounding country and little pen-pictures of the " aeroplane flitting like a dove in the blue sky, surrounded by puffs of snowy smoke " variety, or else *faute de mieux* he recapitulates the salient features of his mother's last letter, dishing it up with an abundance of " wells."

" My dear mother," it generally starts, " your ever-welcome letter to hand. Also the cigs., which were fine. Well, you was saying that Sandy Ross had joined up at last. Well, it's about time he did. Well, this is a nice place but not very warm. Also the women are ugly. Well, little Andy is better, is he ? Tell him I am glad to hear it——" and three pages more in the same vein. I like that sort of letter, there's never anything to censor in it. But I guess the mother likes it more.

Then there's the " old soldier " to his wife. Love for his family runs through an otherwise bald and unconvincing narrative. " Dear wife," he begins, " It was good of you to send the socks as came yesterday. This place is all right, plenty of food, and rum every night. Give my love to Jock and Sally. There is a church here without no steeple which a German shell has blown away. Also little Tom. My officer gave me some cigs. to-day. Not forgetting baby Jean.

Which was good of him. There is a terrible bombardment going on just now, so you might send me another tin of Keatings. I must stop now. And a semmit. Your loving husband. TILL DEATH. No. 13287 Pte. —— xxxxxxxx This for Sally and little Tom xxxx also baby Jean xxxxx. Tell Jock he's got to be a man now and look after you."

Lastly there are the sort you read with one eye shut and the other one looking in the opposite direction. They generally begin, " My own darlingest," etc., etc., and end, " your boy, Jock." On the outside of the envelope are the mystic letters S.W.A.K., but inside there is nothing of military importance.

A certain officer, who shall be nameless, was engaged to a fair young thing. He couldn't write love-letters for nuts, but had in his platoon a certain ex-schoolmaster in the same way as himself. Accordingly he used to copy out the best bits from his school-master's effusions and insert them in his own poor missives. All went well till one day in a fit of absent-mindedness he forgot to change the girl's name. Some people never do have much luck, do they ?

Went into Wipers yesterday and saw the sights. Though half the town is in ruins business is going on more or less as usual. When we were in the cathedral a man in plain clothes started to talk to us in perfect English, and to question us as to the position of the battalion in the trenches. This looked suspish, so when we parted from him I kept watch while my pal went to find the military police. He came back a minute later looking glum. "He says it's only Lord Curzon," was his greeting. Still we did have a good tea.

I'm on a bombing course for a few days now. It's great sport. Beside the ordinary bombs there is a trench howitzer, Minnie by name, fashioned from an old gas-pipe, and a catapult hailing from Gamage's. Neither of them is exactly a weapon of precision, but as toys they take a lot of beating. The first time I ever saw a trench mortar fired was up in the trenches one night. It was loosed off from the back of the trench, and I, in my blissful ignorance, watched it from the fire step, about five yards away and directly in front of it. Later on the same night it burst without warning. I shall know better in future. Some of the bombs are rather priceless, made out of jam tins and stuffed with gunpowder and old iron. You light them with a match, or a cigarette lighter if it's very windy. Five seconds after they are lit they explode. The trouble is that you can't always tell when they are alight.

It's a great life.

Good night.

THOMAS.

THE WAR OFFICE,
FLANDERS,

April 20th.

Why this cottage is called the War Office I may not divulge. It is a pleasant enough spot for a support billet, and on fine days we sit on the grass under the almond blossom and watch the gooseberries grow. There is a ridge between the Germans and ourselves, so we can do this without being spotted. The place always seems just the same. Now it is the cabbages which are beginning to sprout, and now it is the midden which is beginning to smell more middeny than ever, but otherwise nothing changes.

But just across the road, underneath the clump of trees, there is always change. When first we knew the little grass clearing there were two wooden crosses in one corner. Now there must be fifty. Those two graves send a queer thrill through me whenever I see them. The older of the two crosses is bare, save for the inscription :

Ci gît
Pierre Lefroi
Mort pour la patrie
Sept., 1914.

Underneath the other lies a private in the H.A.C. Nailed to the cross is a wreath, a crown of laurel, sent

out from England by his mother " in proud remem-
brance." There they lie side by side, the French *poilu*
and the English gentleman, and who shall say whose
was the greater sacrifice.

We have found a garden full of primroses, and planted
them on the graves of some of our own men. It was
the best we could do for them.

Oh, let's try and be cheerful for a change ! You
should see the food we eat in the trenches. After dark
your batman steals out of the trench and makes his
way to the battered hamlet over the ridge where a few
Belgiques still manage to make a living selling eggs
and tinned stuff. I can't understand how they explain
their needs, but anyhow they do. An hour or so later
a bulky figure lurches in and tries to stow all the newly
bought provender on the small and rickety shelf, which
already groans under the weight of a box of bombs, a
Very pistol, a message pad, and a collection of filthy
sevenpenny books. First a loaf of fresh brown bread,
and then a tin of peaches, followed by half a dozen new
laid eggs (none of your duration-of-the-war-very-
doubtful-variety for my man). As if this wasn't
enough, the next item is a tin of *foie gras*, slightly
rusty outside, but doubtless quite edible. When a
pound of fresh butter follows you hope that this is
the end. But it isn't. My man has his head screwed
on the right way and knows that the more he buys the
more there will be for him to finish up. But when a
sack of potatoes, a bag of biscuits, and some rather
risqué sausages have appeared you really do know

your fate. " That's all I could get," says the universal
provider disappointedly.

His own mother would hardly know her little Thomas
these days, so fat has he grown under the strain of
trench warfare. They are starting to enlarge the
trenches for my benefit.

Last time we were relieved the journey home to our
billets was a distinctly amusing one. The night was
absolutely inky, and everything was slippery from the
incessant rain. The first part of the journey is from
the fire trench back to the road, three-quarters of a
quagmiry mile, the first half of it in full sight of the
flare-loving Hun. The ground is peppered with shell
holes, and seamed with little ditches, all of them full
of ice-cold water. We clambered out of the trench
(I and my platoon) and started on our homeward way.
I led, advancing by inches at a time, and probing the
ground in front with the long pole I always carry at
night for this purpose. Following me were the men,
the foremost gripping me by the coat, and the remain-
der hanging on to the equipment of the man in front.
The rear was brought up by my platoon sergeant, a
cheery soul with no conscience worth writing home
about. Can you imagine us, Phil, stumbling along
through the dark, and falling flat in the mud every
time the star lights went up? There was something in
our antics which reminded me vaguely of a beauty
chorus at its best—you know the way they dance
across the stage and then bob down all together, and
then up and on again. Of course our beauty was

slightly soiled, but what of it ? It's a difficult thing
to fall flat on your face when you are holding on to the
man in front of you, and the man behind is holding on
to you. There is one great disadvantage, too, in being
the leader. Sometimes your pole misses a shell hole.
You don't, and there you are in a cold bath, with a
muffled scream of merriment travelling down the line—
" Th' officer has fell in." Once over the ridge, progress
is much easier, as, instead of ducking when the flares
go up, you pick up your kilts and scuttle, making as
much use as possible of the momentary light, and then
on again at a snail's crawl.

Arrived at the road, we wait shiveringly for the other
three platoons to put in an appearance, and when all
have reported present, start off at the regulation trench
walk of about a mile and a half per hour. Even now
it isn't plain sailing as the road is blocked with transport, but eventually we reach the corner where the
pipers meet us, and where smokes are lighted. Then
grousing voices cease, and sodden feet step out with a
new vigour, and war doesn't seem such a poor game
after all. But no pipes that ever played could guard
against that feeling of utter and complete weariness
which overcomes you as you plod hopelessly along,
half dead and half asleep. All at once the fires of the
cook-house burst into sight and the pipers throw away
their cigarettes and start to fill their pipes with air. To
the regimental march we lurch into camp, trying in a
last effort to keep step to the familiar strains. Rifles
are unloaded, packs thrown off, and the men lie on the

floor of their huts in a coma, while the less fortunate
orderlies hurry off to fetch the dixies of steaming
soup.

Now I'm going to stop as I am just off to play auction. I'm just learning at present, and yesterday lost
my partner seven hundred and thirty points by a
revoke. It seems a good game. I am not playing with
the same man to-day.

Your

THOMAS.

WORM PROSPECT,

April 27th.

Saw a German to-day, Phyllis, the first that has
ever swum into our ken. He must have been walking
along a C.T. (B.E.F. for communication trench) just
as a shell fell in it and closed it up for traffic. Like a
fool he got out and started to walk along the top. Clad
in grey, from his body hung two arms, and he propelled
himself by means of two legs. His face was not wholly
unpleasing, though slightly hairy. So you see, a Hun
isn't really so different from an ordinary human as
some people try and make out. Half a dozen men
started firing rapid at him, and he threw up his hands
and fell into the trench. Guess he was a stretcher case
at the very least. By the way, casualties are divided
up into three classes: walking cases, the slightly
wounded who can get along by themselves ; stretcher
cases, the more seriously hit who have to be taken on

stretchers ; and sandbag cases, where the patient has
to be gathered up and placed tenderly, bit by bit, into
a sandbag or similar receptacle. The third class is the
least popular as no guarantee is given to exclude little
pieces of somebody else from your own particular
sandbag.

Perhaps you have been wondering why this hole has
been christened " Worm Prospect." Well, the reason
is, *tout simple*, that whenever you open your eyes they
light upon a worm, or more frequently worms, gazing
upon you from a hole in the wall and swaying languidly
to and fro, which is all very well, but it rather spoils
your appetite to find a squirmy red body disappearing
into your last tin of condensed milk.

I suppose that you have read about the gas. It
really does seem about the last word in Hunnishness,
doesn't it ? Even we, where we were, were just able
to smell it and our eyes began to water. Incidentally,
too, it is a bit of a nuisance, as since the attack we have
been deluged with conflicting instructions, and things
which the men insist on calling " perspirators."
" B——y perspirators," to be more exact. The first
thing to turn up was a collection of body-belts, that
woolly article of underwear which every British soldier
is supposed to wear round his lower chest, but which
none do wear. These had to be cut up into suitable
lengths and tied over the mouth in case of a gas attack.
Next day we were told that they should be dipped in
hypo, a solution of which should be kept in the trench.
We had to certify that this had been done by midnight

of the same day. Naturally there was none to be got. Next day hypo was a wash-out, and ammonia was all the rage, but it didn't matter much, as there was none of that either. Then along came a new sort of gag, made somewhere down the line, with little tapes hanging all round it. Now we have just had the third variety, a mixture of cotton waste and gauze smeared in something which tastes very nasty. The men don't know where they are. First they are told to breathe in at the mouth and out at the nostrils, and then an order comes cancelling that and recommending the exact opposite. Hardly has the significance of this order been impressed on the men than along sails another *billet-doux* to the effect that the nose should be gripped firmly by the thumb and first finger of the right hand to prevent any air reaching the lungs or being expelled therefrom by way of that limb. Is the nose a limb? Just as you have read this out aloud along comes an orderly with still another missive, to be read to the troops on three successive occasions. According to this the mouth must be firmly closed, and everything done through the nose. Personally, to be quite safe, I have decided not to breathe at all, for if you are caught doing the wrong thing you are liable to be tried by court martial.

The Huns started the second battle of Ypres with a great old bombardo of the town, which was topping to watch—from five miles away. From a hill on which I stood you could see the whole of Belgium which is still in our hands, from Kemmel to the sea. Beautiful green country with row upon row of stately trees just bursting into leaf. Nestling among the trees the red-roofed farm-houses lend a touch of colour to the scene. On every little knoll stands a mill, with sails spread, grinding, grinding, grinding, heedless of the war which is raging only a few miles off. Every here and there a church tower stands out plainly, and away in the distance the white towers of Ypres. As you stand there a huge black cloud rises from the city and covers it as with a pall. Half a minute later you hear a dull roar. Another seventeen-inch missionary of kultur has missed the cathedral. When they started to shell the town it was full of troops, but they have been gone now for several days, as Fritz full well knows, so it looks as if they are pounding the town in sheer spite. One of our officers was just leaving the town when a crump landed in the same street. His horse took seventeen minutes to do the four and a half miles back to camp.

Later. I've just made a prize ass of myself, Phyllis ; such an ass. Just after dark the C.O. came round with a youngish-looking officer, whom I took to be an R.E. He began to criticise a sandbag traverse which my men had built, and which I was rather proud of, and as I was feeling fed up at the time I suggested that the people who lived in the trenches ought to be the best judges of how to build them. " Perhaps you're right," said he, and went off with the C.O.

Soon after the adjutant rang me up and wanted to

know if the C.O. had been round. On my reply that he had—"Well, what did you think of the new general?" came across the phone to me.

Phyllis, I am feeling small. Wish I knew where to hide my diminished head.

Thy
THOMAS.

WARS

CHAPTER II

WARS

THE CAMP IN THE WOOD,
May 10th.

DEAR OLD THING,

I wish you could be here to see this camp. Thirty huts amid the great trees, and all around thickets blazing with purple and gold, hyacinths and primroses. Everywhere the bright new green of spring, and overhead the cloudless blue sky.

We have been here for a week and according to rumour are soon to be in the thick of it. But rumour hasn't proved over-trustworthy of late. The night we left the old trenches for the last time was one of many wild stories. The Germans were into Ypres; we had taken La Bassée; the French were attacking along their whole front with enormous success; Turks had been among the prisoners captured at Hill 60; and as usual Italy had declared war. It's surprising, too, what you will believe if you are in the right mood for it. They say that——

Something's up. We're moving in an hour.

T.

May 17th.

DEAR PHIL,

The alarm was a genuine one after all, and we were away, heading north, not an hour from the time I had to break off my last epistle so hastily. It was a long and dusty march with the pillar of smoke which was Ypres growing ever closer. On the way we passed a battalion, fresh from the place where we were bound. At least it had been a battalion before it had been shelled for three days on end and then gassed. When we saw them they could have best been described as a glorious memory. For the remnant, when they were relieved at last, handed over the same trenches as they had taken over, or rather they handed over the ground on which those trenches had once been. There was a difference in their greeting from that to which we had grown accustomed. " Hope you have a cushy time," it used to be. Now it is, " Give 'em hell, Jocks." Since then we have buried some of their dead and we understand. In fact we have been burying them to-day, burying them with great bunches of lilac tucked into our tunics to lessen the—— but why should I go into all the horrible details. Just one thing, though. Among them, thank God, were some Germans, their purpled faces twisted with agony, and their hands still clutching at their throats in a last vain effort to breathe, victims of their own damnable invention.

We are not actually in the firing line, but live in rat-holes of our own scraping in a railway embankment, half a mile or so to the rear. All night and most of the day we are working at one thing or another, at night carrying rations up to the hill (? what hill), and bringing back rifles, packs, spades, and all the mudded aftermath of a great fight. By day we bury the dead, a horrid job, and not improved by the fact that along the railway you are in full sight of the Hun, though out of effective rifle range.

To reach the much-battered church you have to skirt a lake—at one time the reservoir for Ypres. Round it runs a cinder path, and at one end what was once a cosy little *estaminet* shelters among some trees. Here of a Sunday afternoon the worthy citizen of Ypres was wont to bring his spouse for their weekly constitutional; now an occasional fatigue party slinks along, furtively hugging the bank for cover. Whirring water-fowl skim the surface of the lake, undisturbed save for the occasional plunk into the water of a stray bullet from Hill 60 way. Past the lake you reach the church, standing in the midst of a now deserted village, which was once the headquarters of a cavalry division. We had to clear away the debris— stones, masonry from the tower, jagged iron splinters of the altar rails. The interior was six or seven feet deep in this strange conglomeration, and over all was the sickening, choking dust of smashed and crumbling mortar. As you can imagine, it was some job getting rid of it, but our efforts were rewarded by finding the organ still standing and unharmed. As it happened, X——, who was with me, was by way of being an organist, and soon we had it going. I pumped while X—— played. Can you picture the scene? Away to the west the blood-red sunset seemed but a pale reflection of flaming Ypres. On the other three sides the flare lights were sailing up gently into the gathering darkness, heralds of another night of ceaseless vigil. And from the roofless house of God arose the triumphant swell of the War March from *Athalie*. Before the end the Germans started to whizz bang the village in the hopes of catching a relief going up, and I must confess that I wanted to make myself scarce. But X—— would have none of it. "No d——d Hun is going to make me stop before I want to," he said. And play on he did. Very thrilling and all that for the organist, but not quite so nice for the blower, with plenty of time to think of where the next shell might land. One shell did hit the church, but beyond giving me a fright and covering us in white dust it did us no damage.

Two of my boys had their dug-out blown in on top of them yesterday. At first it looked as if they must have been killed, but we worked like demons to dig them out, in the hopes of finding them still alive. After a quarter of an hour we managed to drag them out, covered with bruises and hardly able to breathe, but whole. We tried artificial respiration, brandy, and all sorts of things. At last they came round, and one of them—we had always thought him a bit of a

weed before—turned round to the other where he lay
and gasped, " Man, yon's gran'. D'ye ken we've
escapit th' efternoon fatigue."

Which is more than I can manage to do.

So, farewell.

Your

THOMAS.

THE BE-UTIFUL CAMP,

May 22nd.

DEAR PHIL,

I sent you some souvenirs to-day, done up in a
sandbag and labelled " officer's surplus kit." I hope
that they will reach you all right. The shell-case is an
18-pdr. one, appropriated from a pile sent to us for
use as gas alarms. It has a beautiful deep note and
would do splendidly for a dinner-gong. There are
several German nose-caps. We picked them up by
handfuls just behind Hill 60. What looks like a bit
of a broken bottle is in reality stained glass from one
of the shattered windows of Ypres Cathedral. I wonder
if the lily of the valley will still be recognisable. It
comes from the garden of the *padre* of Zillebeke, and
was growing on the lip of an enormous shell hole. The
lace collar was made at Ypres just before the second
battle. At least I bought it as such from the good dame
who said she made it, but for all I know it may have
had Birmingham as its birthplace. That's the lot I
think.

We've had a new sub posted to the company, and to me has fallen the honour of instructing him in trench warfare. He was a pleasant addition to a dug-out I can tell you. His mouth is large and admirably suited to the method of mastication favoured by him. His hair is of a nondescript shade, best describable as " dirty sandbag," and his eyes are small and pig-like. When he walks his hands flop about like washing in the wind, except that washing is generally clean. His conversation centres round the abnormal percentage of casualties among officers, and every sentence is rounded off with an " eh ? " only to be equalled by the bleat of an epileptic lamb.

Lloyd George claims that silver bullets are going to win the war. According to Lord Northcliffe it is high explosives which will at last enable us to blast our way to Berlin. Others mention the Navy, the Russian steam-roller, the liquor restrictions, and what not. I once heard a man say that the brains of the Staff would be the deciding factor, but I am not such a pessimist as he. I still hope for a favourable issue. The man who is going to win the war is the poor old lance-corporal of the unpaid variety. General A wants something done. He acquaints Col. B of his wishes. Col. B notifies Capt. C, who in his turn passes on the good news to 2nd Lieut. D, who skilfully shifts the burden to Sergt. E. Sergt. E, intent on obtaining a disproportionately large issue of rum for his platoon and himself, details Lance-corp. (unpaid) F. Lance-corp. (unpaid) F takes six men, three shovels, a pick, and a tin of chloride of lime, and the job gets done. Then he returns and reports the completion of the job to Serg. E. Sergt. E steps up to 2nd Lieut. D, salutes, and reports—" I've done that job, sir." " I " mark you. No mention of Lance-corp. (unpaid) F, with his six men, three shovels, pick, and tin of chloride of lime. 2nd Lieut. D wires to Capt. C, " Have done job." Capt. C sends a message by orderly to the effect that he, " he " mark you, has completed the allotted task. Col. B takes pen in hand and writes, " Ref. your B.M. 3427 I beg to report that this work has been brought to a satisfactory conclusion by me." Still no word of Lance-corp. (unpaid) F. General A, replete with a good dinner, receives the message. " Good fellow that Col. B," he murmurs. In due course Col. B becomes Col. B, c.m.g. Lance-corp. (unpaid) F remains Lance-corp. (unpaid) F, until a kindly shell carries his head away.

We straggled home to camp two days ago, picking our way among the shell holes by the flickering light of the fires of Ypres. It was good to be back.

Good night.

Your

Thomas.

HELL FIRE CORNER,

June 2nd.

DEAR PHIL,

These are strenuous times indeed. It's well over a week since we came up here, and this is the first opportunity I have had of getting off a letter.

We had rather a thrilling march up, and made all the more thrilling by the probability of having to make an attack at the end of it. We felt rather like making one after what we had seen on Hill 60, and we should have had to do it, too, only something went wrong with the Staff work.

Along the none too wide road four streams of traffic were passing. On the outside, to the right, were we marching out. Jostling us, and moving in the same direction, clattered long lines of ammunition limbers, British and Belgian, the latter reminiscent of country bakers' carts manned by semi-equipped emergency postmen. With them went convoys of motor-ambulances. Coming the other way the same limbers and ambulances, but now the limbers were empty and the ambulances full. And on the far side of the road straggling little groups of weary men, some of them hardly able to breathe from the effects of the gas. Through it all buzzed the dispatch riders, twisting and turning among the horses with unbelievable skill. As we marched the men sang, sang as only

Scotch troops can, snatches from Harry Lauder chiefly, strangely beautiful, despite their music-hall origin, and fine tunes to march to. The troops bivouacked just off the road, crowded on to its grass border and watched us pass. " Ullo, Jocks," cried one humorist. " Ahve seen a good few battalions march up that way, but preshus few come back." Which, though true, was hardly cheering, was it ?

Gradually the traffic began to thin out, but we carried on, the men still singing :

> . . . So don't cry, dear,
> I'm a'richt here.
> It's just like being at hame.
> One two, three, WE DON'T THINK !

After a time we were alone, save for two " Archies " and their attendant ammunition lorry. There is something very attractive about their curiously shaped guns, which look for all the world like giant triple telescopes. Then a great grey armoured car whizzed by, the Dreadnought of the land, with R.N. in large red letters on its body, bringing with it a breath of ozone.

At last we reached the outskirts of Ypres. At the bridge where the sentry stands, guarding the ruined city from the hand of the looter, the pipers turned aside and broke into " Hielan' Laddie." From the men came what a journalist would probably describe as a " deep-throated roar," and for the life of me I can't give a better word for it. In it blended the voices

of the business men, students, clerks, artisans, farm
labourers, stevedores, and all the other classes which
go to make up the battalion. As we entered Wipers it
died down, for who could be aught but silent in that city
of the dead? Past the Cloth Hall, past the Cathedral,
past shops and houses now little heaps of crumbling
brick, through the Menin Gate, across the moat, and
out into the Salient.

The men we relieved had been cut up even worse
than the Hill 60 lot, and as they had been driven back
by the gas we found ourselves taking over open positions behind hedges instead of trenches. The men, of
course, were dead fagged by the time they got there,
but we had to set them to dig themselves in without a
moment's rest. Poor devils. But at dawn we were
so far down that the Hun had only our head and
shoulders to pot at instead of our entire weary anato-
mies.

Since then we have spent the time being shelled by
their artillery—yesterday we had thirteen hours of it
without a moment's respite. By night we try to
rebuild the trenches which have been blown in by day.
After the Germans have been shelling us for an hour
or so our own artillery will reply with one round of
shrapnel, generally a " dud." But of course that isn't
their fault. If only the B.E.F. could lay hands on the
man whose fault it is, he would have a pretty rough
crossing.

Was out in No Man's Land last night firing rifle
grenades. It was creepy work out there in the long,

wet grass, in which you kept on running against dead bodies. To my dismay they all failed to explode, and it was not till we got back safely that I remembered that I had not pulled out the pins! And at a guinea a time that's hardly helping to win the war, is it?

We hear (1) that our depleted battalion is shortly to return home to recruit, (2) that all T.F. battalions are to be withdrawn from the firing line, (3) that we are to do an attack, (4) that we are to form the nucleus of a new conscript battalion, (5) that we are going to Rouen to dig drains.

There's a fine selection for you. Take your choice and it's certain to be untrue. Meanwhile here are we stretched across the road to Ypres, and holding what is probably the most important part of the whole line.

With which cheery thought, farewell.

Your

Tired THOMAS.

SAME PLACE,

June 12th.

CHÉRIE (French),

Still here, and no word of being relieved. That's only nineteen days that we've been in the front line without a relief, and we haven't lost more than two hundred men during the time, so we aren't doing so badly.

All the same, life's hardly worth living. From dewy dawn till the stars begin to peep the Hun shells us, shell after shell the whole day long, and we just have to sit and look pleasant. Our own artillery do their best, but all they can do is to polish their guns and think how nice it would be to have something to fire out of them. If only we could have the man here who said that there was no shortage of shells.

I'm not being very cheerful, am I, but at present I'm suffering rather badly from lack of sleep. This morning after " stand to " I told my servant to make me a cup of cocoa. Before it was ready I had fallen asleep and he had to wake me. I took the cocoa from him and tried to drink it, but it was too hot, and so I sat down and waited for it to cool. I must have fallen off again directly, as I woke up with a start to find scalding liquid trickling down my kilt and on to my bare knees. I didn't want to let my man see what a fool I had made of myself, so I raked up an old Tommy's Cooker and put a dixie of water on it. My dug-out was on fire when I woke up again, and I had to use all my remaining water to put it out. After this I gave up all idea of a hot drink and went to sleep on the sopping floor of the dug-out. Five or six hours later a small earthquake roused me to the fact that all around me was dark. This was astonishing for midday in June. A shell had closed up the dug-out door, an ungentlemanly thing to do, but better perhaps than coming in through

the door. When my men dug me out they told me
that this sort of thing had been going on for over
an hour, and that they had retired to the far end
of the trench, and had wondered why I didn't do
likewise.

You remember me giving you a lengthy account of
a most obnoxious fellow, don't you? Well, he has
left us. His going was thus. One of our positions, an
advanced one, is some distance ahead of the rest, and
listening posts have to be placed all round it by night.
My pet aversion went out to visit them last night, as
it was his tour of duty. He should have known where
they were, but apparently he did not, for he managed
somehow or another to walk right through them unseen. Coming back though he was spotted and, very
naturally, taken for a Hun. The listening post started
to loose off at him, as they could get no answer to their
challenge, and he, thinking that he had been ambushed,
started to reply with his revolver. Between them they
must have expended between fifty and a hundred
cartridges before our young hero was hit in the arm.
He then beat a hasty retreat, and burst into the west
end of the trench with his story of an ambush at the
same time that the listening post crawled over the
parapet at the east end, raising the alarm and declaring
that they had driven back a strong enemy recon-
noitring party with heavy loss.

Later.—I've been hit, Phyllis, and am feeling a
regular wounded 'ero. I was walking along the trench

when there was a bang, and I was thrown forward on to my face. " You're hit, sir, hit in the back," said one of my men, and with a breathless haste my tunic and shirt was torn off, to disclose a shrapnel ball clinging lovingly to my spine in the midst of a huge bruise. The skin had just been scratched. Oh, I was sick. I had fully expected a nice cushy one, and a month down the line, with perhaps a fortnight's sick leave in England to top up with, and then to find it was the merest scratch. Oh, it was cruel. However, the news got round, and I had a message from battalion H.Q. asking whether they should send along a stretcher ! And when I went down to the dressing station to get some iodine put on the wound the M.O. turned round to the orderly and said, " Just put some iodine on this officer's wound, will you. You'll find it if you look long enough." That put the lid on it. No more wounds for me.

Till next time,

Your wounded hero,

THOMAS.

STILL THE SAME SPOT,

June 18th.

This is a great life, Phyllis, if it wasn't for the death. We have been in our first show, and for the last twenty-four hours have been shaking hands with ourselves at still being in the land of the living. I had a good look at myself this morning in my steel pocket mirror, but failed to discover any grey hairs or fresh furrows of care across my forehead. That wasn't surprising, though, as the mirror has become so rusty that it takes some time to find out what part of your face is being reflected in it.

You will probably have read by now that our line was advanced along the Menin Road on a front of so much and to a depth of so much.

Our battalion was not in the charge, but was holding the trenches from which it was made. It was just as well, as the men could hardly be described as in the best of health after twenty-three days in the front line without a really healthy drink all the time. [The water that comes up to us every night is a sickly brown, doped with chlorate of lime to kill the weaker microbes.] Anyhow we got it in the neck a bit, as the Germans shelled us hard the whole time the show was going on, and one company had to go up and consolidate the captured line, and lost a lot on the way up.

The attack was made at dawn and was heralded by the first real bombardment put up by our guns. For half an hour the shells were just tumbling over each other in a wild rush to get to the German trenches, and then one of the other brigades in the division went over the top. As they went our men stood on the parapet and cheered them on. It was a great sight, and you quite forgot to notice that the shells were falling around you too. An eight-inch crump descended on our trench and hit the parapet, covering the veteran of the platoon with earth, but failing to explode. Which was just as well for all concerned, as an eight-inch crump is no laughing matter. The veteran picked himself up and indulged in a selection from those expressions so dear to the heart of the " old soldier." When he had finished his face lit up in a grin. " Eh, but I cud dee wi' a seat fine," and he sat himself down calmly on the dud and went on looking at the attacking line, which we could just see clambering into the first line of German trenches.

A few minutes later, as we were all talking excitedly in our trench, one of the sentries cried out, " Here come the Gairmans," and when I jumped up on to the fire step to have a look there they were, advancing in mass towards us. By now all the men were manning the parapet waiting for the order to fire, which I was keeping back until the Huns were right up to the wire. Suddenly I noticed something about them. They were unarmed. Then it struck me that they must be prisoners, but there was no sign of any guard. Down the road they came in fours running to beat the wind, evidently wanting to get away from the ñasty war as soon as possible. At least a hundred yards behind them came their guard, one man in full equipment with a rifle on which was fixed a red-tipped bayonet. On his head a German helmet. Weighed down by his arms and booty he was utterly unable to keep up with his charges, and as he passed us was steadily losing ground. You should have heard him puffing by, anathematising breathlessly the over-eagerness of his flock. We sank into the bottom of the trench and shook with laughter for five minutes. I don't mind if I never see a more amusing sight. One of the men as he passed waved his hand to us and shouted in English, " Back to goot old Lunton."

All the wounded came back through our trench. It would have been rather a ghastly sight had it not been for the delight which showed plainly on the faces of most of the men to be going home to Blighty. All of them were tremendously excited ; this man wanted to show you just how he killed two fleeing Teutons with one jab ; that man couldn't stop talking of the hot coffee they had found up in the German lines. Quite a thousand passed through during the day.

K.'s Army put in an appearance for the first time that afternoon.

We lost about a hundred men during the show, which lasted till night, so altogether we have lost getting on for half our men since we came up here. It looks as if they must relieve us soon. This is our twenty-fifth day in, and as you can see I've been reduced to writing to you on pink message forms.

Good-bye.

Your freely perspiring

THOMAS.

P.S.—Excuse the finger-marks, but I haven't had a real wash for eleven days, or a bath for fifty-five. Isn't it a terrible war ?

IN BIVOUAC,

June 21st.

At last ! After the twenty-six longest days in the world we have been relieved. Our relief belonged to the newly out " Great citizen army," which, from reading the papers of the last four months, we had begun to believe to be a collection of supermen. But they aren't, they're just ordinary people. It came as a bit of a disappointment, though, to find that they, like ourselves, felt tired at the end of a ten-mile march along dusty roads, wearing full equipment, and it was still more disheartening to learn that our machine gunners, despised Terriers, were to stay in a few days longer to stiffen the line. However, we got away, which was the main thing.

We are bivouacked in a field, a few tents for the officers and two blankets between four men for bivvies. It isn't much cover, but it's not so bad while the weather is good. We've got a gramophone, and we're quite near a little village where you can get champagne at 3f. 50 a time. So we're all right. The gramophone was smashed to bits on the way out, and you are sick if you drink the champagne. But we're all right.

The men have seized the opportunity of being near a village to go and buy post cards to send home. A few of them go in for pictures of Ypres after the second bombardment, or the church of Dickebusch—isn't Dickebusch a topping name ?—or the square at Poperinghe, or some other equally enthralling view. These they may send home on condition that the name of the place is deleted. To delete is apparently short for " to place one very light pencil mark through," to judge from some of the efforts at deletion. As usual, though, it is the fault of one of the great tribe of Brass Hats. If he had omitted the word delete in his lengthy circular upon the subject and substituted " scratch out " all would have been well, but you can't very well punish a man for not understanding his own language.

More popular than the " View " is what I call the " Allies in Arms " type, in which sheer realism and artistic reproduction are combined with stupendous success. As a rule five figures are posed in attitudes of defiance upon the centre of a highly glazed card. Sometimes there are only four, sometimes the production is upon a lavish scale and there are six. But the number is quite immaterial. What does matter though is the fact that these figures represent the four, five, or six allies, as the case may be, united against the common foe. Indeed two lines of French doggerel below inform the ignorant of this glorious fact, if he can read French that is. Of course, to those versed in military uniforms as seen at revues, not reviews, the matter would be one of no great difficulty. In the centre a form in baggy red trousers and blue coat could easily be mistaken by the initiated for a French *poilu*, even were it not for the sham beard which he, or on looking closer perhaps it's a she, is wearing. Supporting the central figure on the right is a warrior of somewhat mixed origin. The upper half seems to belong to a British sailor, but the khaki trousers and puttees are unmistakably those of a Tommy. Here again the shape of the leg underneath the puttee lends weight to the supposition that female labour is being employed. On the left is Russia, resplendent in green overcoat, furry cap, gum boots, and again the imitation beard. On the wings are Belgium, in gaily tasselled *képi*, and a nondescript figure which will do for Serbia, Japan, or Montenegro, according to taste. The whole are armed with the very latest pattern rifles from the toyshop department of the nearest Bon Marché. The colouring is gorgeous, not only of the figures but also of the background, which is either a shipwreck or a battle (it is hard to decide which) painted on a sheet. The price which one has to pay for this work of art is one penny. Isn't it wonderful how they do it ?

You can hardly imagine after what I have just described that there can be anything more thrilling in the post card line. But there is. It is the woolly post card. You can buy them at any shop in Belgium, at any house almost. Conjure up in your mind what an old-fashioned Valentine would have looked like if it had been condensed into the size of a post card, make all the colours three times as vivid, mix them in one gorgeous riot of bad taste, and add an expression of

the deepest affection, in French, and then you will
have a faint idea of the woolly post card. Take for
instance the one sent by my servant the other day to
his former " meenister." In the centre two hands of
purple silk were clasped in loving friendship. Just
below them a green and a mauve heart nestled coyly,
their colours blending splendidly with a wreath of
pink, yellow, and blue flowers which surrounded the
card. In the right hand top corner was the tricolour,
and balancing it on the left was an embryonic Union
Jack. Evidently the careless worsted worker, or whoever it is that does this sort of thing, was a bit shaky
on the composition of our complicated national em-
blem. You could recognise it though. Across the
bottom of the card was written in letters of golden silk,
" Je t'aime, chérie." I wonder how the parson liked
that.

The following story is guaranteed true by my platoon
sergeant. I have known more truthful men than he is
apt to be when fact looks like spoiling fiction. Up in
the trenches there was one spot only about fifteen
yards from the Hun, and here some of the leading
humorists of the platoon used to forgather of a
morning to indulge in *badinage* with similarly minded
Huns across the way. One day the sanitary man—a
very witty fellow I am led to believe—had a brain
wave. After a certain amount of wordy warfare he
adopted a more serious tone, and informed the
Germans that they must behave well on the morrow as
certain members of the Coalition Cabinet were to make

a tour of the trenches. Next day the humorists proceeded along the trench bearing on the end of sticks a variegated selection of headgear boned from Ypres, top-hats, bowlers, and the more humble felt hat. As they went they hurrahed loudly, with the intention of making the Hun think that the Ministers were being shown round. To their disappointment nothing happened. They had expected at the very least showers of bombs (some people have a remarkable sense of humour), shells, and perhaps with luck the " Hymn of Hate." But nothing happened. After the demonstrations were over the incensed sanitary man got into communication with his friends the enemy and asked them if they hadn't noticed the Cabinet going round. Yes they had spotted the line of hats bobbing along, and had heard the resounding cheers. Why then hadn't they done anything ? The reply was crushing. " Why for should ve our best vriends to kill want ? " As I have said, my sergeant's information is not always reliable. Also he is a confirmed reader of *John Bull* and of the " Paper which foretold the war," and doesn't love Asquith and Co. At any rate I never heard the cheering, and I very much doubt if the Germans could understand the remarks of the sanitary man, who hails from one of the remotest islands in the Hebrides and speaks a language of his own.

I shall have to stop now as battalion mess is in five minutes. We still feed together whenever possible, though there was a distinct movement in favour of company messes the other night after the newly appointed mess sergeant, a balloon vendor in peace time, had smothered the macaroni cheese with sugar.

Cheero.

THOMAS.

P.S.—There is some word of leave starting soon.

June 29th.

FIELD POST OFFICE TELEGRAM

VICTORIA 2.30 P.M. TO-MORROW

THOMAS

THE WITCHES' CAULDRON

CHAPTER III

THE WITCHES' CAULDRON

CAMP,

July 12th.

DEAR PHIL,

Said I was going to be ill crossing over, didn't I ? Well, I was. It was pretty rough, but I managed to withstand the dread complaint remarkably well until we passed the leave boat homeward bound. That, and the memory of seven days of high living, and the anticipation of many months of dirty water and bully beef, was too much for me, and I succumbed.

I dropped a bit of a brick, by the way, getting to Victoria so early, as a kind-looking old fellow, with R.T.O. on his arm, sidled up to me and asked for my name. Being of a trustworthy nature, I gave him the right one, whereupon he told me that he detailed me as a conducting officer, and that I should be responsible for a batch of the men in the train and on the boat. With two others, similarly ensnared, I travelled down in the second train, the one without the Pullman, and so missed my breakfast. It was not very clear to any of us what we were meant to do, so we did nothing. Every one seemed quite satisfied, and got off the train and on to the boat without any assistance, nor did there appear to be anything for us to do on the boat until we reached France, when there was a call for " Conducting officers." I went up on deck and found the landing officer instructing my fellow-unfortunates to march the men up to a camp five miles out of Boulogne. There seemed to be quite a lot of them to do the job, and they looked fairly capable, so I escaped downstairs and snored hard until all the men were off the boat. On the homeward journey I was equally badly had. Some of us, thinking ourselves very cunning, rushed off the train and on to the quay. There we found a fine cross-channel steamer drawn up, but did not notice that on the other side of her was a very old and dingy-looking boat. The gangways were not down when we arrived, but on seeing us a kind skipper man (or so we thought him at the time) had one let down for us. We hopped on, and he had the gangway pulled up again. Then he told us that he had a job for us. We were to travel on the dingy old tub, in charge of the men. " It starts first," he threw at us, as we gloomily transferred our belongings thither. Yes, it started first. But it reached Blighty an hour and a half after the proper boat. In future we shall know better. When travelling in France it is a sound rule to keep away from anyone with a coloured band round his arm. It does not mean that he is infectious, or even that he has been vaccinated lately. But it does mean that he is dangerous.

The journey from Boulogne up the line was quite the

most dismal affair imaginable. Seven of us crowded into a very doubtful third-class carriage, and all of us as gloomy, depressed, and tired as could be. That journey makes you wonder whether leave is worth while.

At H—— we had to get out and change. We were told by the R.T.O. that our train started at 5 a.m. It was 4.30 at the time, so we invaded an *estaminet* and persuaded the patron to let us have coffee and something in it which is strictly *défendu*. At 4.55 we returned to the station to see the train puffing out of the station. This was unheard of. For a train to start late is taken as a matter of course. For a train to start punctually elicits comment. But for a train to start before time was unheard of, a disgrace to the British Army, and many other unprintable things. So we adjourned to the office of the R.T.O. and spoke to him on the matter in terms of honeyed sweetness. He was a blasé young man with an eye-glass through which he gazed at us inquisitively. At last he gathered that we were complaining about his train service, and this seemed to annoy him. " Well, you know, you fellows," he exclaimed, " I weally don't wun this wotten wailway. It's pwetty pwiceless for a felloe to get wagged like this because the twain's gone. I'm not the engine dwiver." After all we found that it wasn't the 5 o'clock train that we had seen steaming out, but the 12.15, four and three-quarter hours late. We eventually caught the 5 o'clock at 10.17, and got to camp to find the battalion back in it from the trenches.

The other evening we had a concert out in the fields, squatting round a large and brightly burning bonfire. These impromptu concerts are great fun, except perhaps for the songsters. The performer stands on the driving seat of a wagon and clears his throat huskily. His friends make encouraging remarks, and offer useful suggestions. All power of song seems to have left him, as he stands there, a prey to stage fright of the most virulent kind. At last he gathers up courage and starts a low moaning, gradually rising in tone until he has attained the desired key. This seems the favourite way of doing it in the absence of a piano. Once started, the song, which is of the ultra-pessimistic " cheild-your-father-has-gown-down-in-the-good-ship-Queen-Bess " type, seems unending, verse succeeding verse with regular monotony. You sit and pray for the end and wonder whether the singer is doing it consciously or not. When at last he does stop the applause is simply terrific, for there is nothing in the musical line which the British soldier prefers to a good old mournful dirge. Warmed up by the clapping, the artist breaks forth into another rollicking ditty of some fourteen verses. This time the poor child has lost her mother, who has " broken her veow," whatever that may be, and so the poor child, to make it rhyme properly, " has no meother neow." More applause greets this effort, but now that the child is both fatherless and motherless the singer seems to have lost interest, and jumps down from the wagon, and retires to nurse his grief in the transport lines. He is followed by a piper, who plays an eightsome reel, whereupon the more energetic and light-footed members of the audience take unto themselves partners and dance. Against the light of the fire and with the swinging kilts and blood-curdling " Heuchs," the whole scene might have been taken from the heart of the Fiji Islands. When the pipes have died down and the weary dancers have sunk to the ground, a small figure mounts the wagon and without any fuss at all starts on his song. He is a devotee of Harry Lauder and rolls out the rrrrr-laden lines in a way which would do credit to that famous man. The men join in the choruses with vigour, and the sounds of revelry must easily reach the village close by.

> Just a wee Deoch an' Doris,
> Just a wee'n, that's a',
> Just a wee Deoch an' Doris
> Before we gang awa'

sounds none the worse for the fact that we, in this pestilential land, are far from the home of the D. and D. When he is too hoarse to sing any longer the would-be Lauder gives way to a serious-looking youth from the signallers. He coughs twice to claim attention and then starts off in resounding tones, " Gunga Din. The tale of a bhisti." Oh, heavens, I wish some law could be passed forbidding the recital of that thing. I think I've heard it at every concert I've been to since the beginning of the war. He, too, ends at last, after having topped his first piece with " Deadwood Dick, a tale of the Rocky Mountains." Next comes a quartet, well sung, about a rather doubtful character named Samuel

Hall, and the quartet are succeeded by a throaty tenor with the inevitable " Keep the Home Fires Burning." The quartermaster gives a little juggling ; our quarter-master can juggle with anything, from ration indents up. His juggling would have been more effective had not the bonfire by this time burnt very low. Still he is popular, and everyone cheers him heartily. Eight Platoon's band then takes a turn at rag-time melodies. They are rather good considering that they possess one melodeon, a Japanese violin, three mouth-organs, and a biscuit tin. Pte. Melhuish, formerly of Binks and Jinks, the world-famed knock-about comedians, is the star turn of the evening. He comes on next and sings a version of " The little grey home in the West," which he proudly informs you is his own handiwork. The exact nature of the parody need hardly be gone into, but it may give you an inkling to say that West has been changed to vest, and after our experiences in those last trenches the song has a touch of homeliness in it which makes it go down splendidly. For an encore he sings that well-known patriotic air, " I want to go home." I wonder what the Germans would think of our moral if they could hear seven hundred men sing-ing as one :

> . . . where the Alleyman can't catch me.
> Oh ! My ! I don't want to die. I want to go home.

The concert ended with the *padre* singing " Annie Laurie " and " Will ye no come back again," and then it was time for the men to retire to their blanket bivvies and sleep. A bit of a change after last week's revues and comedies, wasn't it ?

Now I must away, as I have taken on the job of bombing officer, and have seventy trusty " boomers," as they call themselves, to train.

Cheero.

THOMAS.

CAMP,

July 24th.

PHYLLIS MINE,

Just back from our second show. We went up on the evening of the 18th, knowing nothing of what was in store for us, and twenty-four hours later were pitchforked into as uncomfortable a spot as could be found anywhere upon this earth.

About 4 o'clock on the 19th I was turning in for my first nap since the morning of the day before when an orderly came along to tell me that I was wanted at H.Q. There I obtained the pleasant nformation that the battalion on the left were to attack at dusk, and occupy a large crater that was to be substituted for a German strong point, with the aid of two tons of explosives and to the detriment of its Hunnish garrison. My bombers were to create as much of a diversion as possible with rifle grenades, trench mortars, and other forms of frightfulness. So instead of any sleep I had to go up to the posts again and get ready our perform-ance. At one point our trenches approached very

close to the enemy's, and here we put our trench
mortar, one of the famous gas-pipe type which I have
already described to you. Along the rest of the front
line were bombers with rifle grenades, waiting for the
mine to go up. At seven o'clock exactly there was a
terrific crash. The trench rocked to and fro and seemed
to be on the point of falling in. Away on the top of
the ridge, five hundred yards to our left, the whole
earth seemed to rise in the shape of a big bell, black
with great spurts of flame running through it. Then
as the earth subsided, and while we were listening to
catch the first sounds of the falling debris, our guns
opened out, several hundred of them in a few seconds.
We had never seen anything like it before, so intense
was the bombardment and so confined were its limits.
As the guns opened fire my trench mortar came into
action. It sounds much more important to say " came
into action " than the more commonplace " pooped
off." Up, up, it went through the trees, and down with
a thud into the German trench opposite. It was a
tremendously lucky shot. With a contemptible little
" pop " it exploded, at least it sounded contemptible
amidst all the thunder of the guns. My observer came
rushing down from his post, his face flushed with excitement, and shouted out that we had bagged a
German officer, who had been exposing himself to look
at the commotion which had suddenly arisen on his
flank. Of course I didn't believe him, as trench mortar
enthusiasts are even more egregious liars than snipers.
However, he stuck to his tale, and even insisted on the

officer. Eventually he persuaded me to come and look for myself. When we got to the observation post we peered out of the loop-hole, and he pointed out to me the place where the parapet had been partly blown away by the hit. "Got that, sir?" he went on. "Well then, five yards to the right, that bush out in front of their trench." I looked, and there sure enough was the grey and red peaked cap of a German officer. Some shot, wasn't it? We went on firing for another hour or so, and occasionally had the luck to secure a direct hit, but no such tangible proof of success was awarded us again. A message came through that we had won the position, and soon after, as everything seemed quiet, I retired to my dug-out in the hope of snatching an hour's rest, but to no purpose, as almost at once an orderly came panting with a message that all bombs and bombers were wanted on the left at once, as the bombs were running out and the bombers who took part in the attack had mostly become casualties. Off I went again, and in half an hour my sergeant was away with eight men, and as many bombs as they could carry. An hour later the rest of them were ready, and off we went, leaving our own trenches bomb and bomberless. It was a nice sensation going up to that crater, something like walking in your own funeral procession. When we reached it, after passing through a deadly sort of barrage with amazing luck, the crater was an awful sight. By the light of the moon you could see it all, the great yawning hole, a good fifty feet deep, with dead bodies stretched in ghastly attitudes down its steep sides. Every now and then one of the bodies, stirred by some explosion, would turn over and roll to the bottom, sliding down into a perfect shambles, where it would soon lose its identity among the jumbled heap of corpses and shattered limbs. Around the lip of the crater our men were trying to dig themselves in, but the earth was no firmer than sand, and in a second the crumbling foundations of an hour's desperate work would slide to the bottom, where at least they helped to cover up the awfulness which the first light of dawn was beginning to show up still more clearly. At one or two points, where old trenches led up to the crater, heavy bombing was going on, and it was only with the greatest difficulty that the enemy was being kept back. Our job was not in the crater just then and so we clambered over the lip and into another bit of trench which had been captured by us for some length, after which the Germans were still in possession. When we arrived, the first sight that met us was my bombing sergeant, lying dead on the top of the parapet. He had thrown all the bombs that he and his men had brought up, and then, when they had run out, and no more were to be had, he had climbed up on to the parapet and, in full sight of the German second line eighty yards away, had fired at their bombing parties as they tried to work up the front line trench towards them. He had kept them off like this for twenty minutes, standing up there amidst an ever-growing hail of bullets. Then he fell, shot through the heart. But his work had been done. Either he had caused so many casualties among the enemy's bombers that they were unable to come on or else he had scared them so badly that they dared not. Anyhow they did not, and our arrival with several hundred more bombs came just in time. But for him it would have been too late. We buried him that evening, but by next morning all signs of his grave had disappeared as the result of the bombardment to which we were subjected all that night. And it was a bombardment too. Every German gun for miles around seemed to be trying to hit the same spot, the spot on which I was standing too. They evidently meant to attack us, but our guns also got going, and so accurately that nothing could have lived along the battered bit of trench between the Germans and us. Luckily the Hun had over-estimated the range by a dozen yards or so, and when daylight came it found us still there, but the ground just behind us torn up and torn up again by the unending tornado of shells. One thing we have learnt by that night and that is that as long as you can hear the shells falling singly whzzz-kerump, whzzzz-kerump you probably feel in the most awful funk and wish you were dead, but when the shells are so thick around you that the explosions have become one roar, and you have no time to think that the next one is sure to get you, then the feeling of funk gives way to one of a sort of elation. Still, give me the place where shells are unknown.

I established myself in a dug-out, through the floor of which a mine shaft had been sunk to a depth of some seven or eight feet, and during "stand to" in the morning, a time when every one must be awake, I went into the dug-out and sat down on an ammunition box to write a report. I woke up three hours later, standing in the bottom of the mine shaft. How I got there Heaven alone knows. While I must have been sleeping down there the corporal who has taken my sergeant's place came in to look for me, and of course could not see me. He went out and sent men round the trenches to look for me, but no trace could he find, and so he reported me " missing, believed killed " !

We were relieved after two days of it, and returned to the trenches in the wood, which seemed a second heaven after that horrible crater. Next day the battalion was relieved, once more by Kitchener people, and we reached camp with the milkman, very weary but rather pleased with ourselves.

To keep myself awake on the night of the twentieth I had to resort to writing poetry. Here is the result :

> At tea-time in the trench one day
> A shell took Bailey's brain away;
> Said Thomas as he cut the bread,
> " Look, there goes poor old Billy's head."

And

> Walking heedless through the slush
> To the neck sank Private Rush,
> Shouting, " If you pass this place,
> Keep your damned boots off my face."

Your

THOMAS.

A HOME FROM HOME,

July 30th.

DEAR PHIL,

As I may have remarked before, this is indeed a terrible war. About a week ago we relieved a battalion which had been in the same trenches for exactly one hundred days without relief. Isn't it just awful to think of. A hundred days of what might be described as a " hell upon earth." It might also be described, in the words of the song, as " A little bit of heaven." When they heard that they were to be relieved can you not imagine the sighs of relief, the cries of joy, the eager looking forward to the moment when they could once more turn their backs to the trenches and be at rest? You may think you can. But you can't. When the colonel in command of the little band of heroes heard of the impending relief what he really said was, " Oh ———," and if the colonel so far forgot himself as to say that, what must the men have said ? For this place is a perfect paradise. On either side of it, and not half a mile distant, are two of the hottest spots in the salient, automatic corpse factories. But here there is peace. And the extraordinary thing about it is that we are closer to the Hun than we have ever been before. There is not a single spot in the whole of our front line which is more than seventy yards from the Germans, and the average distance is about forty. It almost seems as if the higher command of either side had forgotten about it altogether, and as long as they will continue to do so we feel convinced that we are just suited for the part of defenders of the Bl—— I nearly let the cat out of the bag then, didn't I ?

There are three lines of good trenches with dug-outs for all the men, a new experience for us. They are on the further edge of a forest of larch, and the soil is sandy and the air invigorating. Of course they have an easterly aspect, but this is war, and we are willing to put up with a small inconvenience like that. From the front lines communication trenches run downhill, through patches of purple heather, to battalion H.Q. where I live these days. Here I share a most gorgeous apartment with the machine gun officer. Several steps take you down to it from ground level, and you enter by a real door. Inside, the first thing to note is a real window, complete with glass, and two good imitations of beds, made of wood and canvas. The walls are lined with canvas, thereby excluding the vagrant worm, and pictures of Gaby Deslys in varying stages of deshabille look down at you with welcoming smiles from the roof. The next thing you notice is that you are standing upright without hitting your head against anything, and then an uncommon feeling of firmness underfoot testifies to the fact that the floor is of brick. There is a pump close by where clean water can be obtained, and the Hun, in moments of wildest fury, has been known to throw over one small shell into a deserted part of the wood. This is the life ! The only little trouble is trench mortars. We have a new sort of engine up in the support line which throws giganlic leaden footballs with tails in the direction of the Hun. These seldom explode, but the suspense or something is too much for Fritz, who replies enthusiastically with smaller but more efficient projectiles. Taken in small doses, even this can be turned into a kind of round game. The bombs always fall in or near the same place, the Playground by name. This is a rather feeble bit of trench with a small hollow in the ground running along behind it. In this hollow we can run about and play without danger of being sniped at by the Hun. When he starts to serenade us with the local *Minenwerfer*, or Minnehahas as they are more commonly known, we ups and outs on to the Playground, and wait for the next to come over. There is a " poof " and there up in the air, for all the world like a big beer bottle on the loose, is the latest little bit of hate. Up, up, up it goes and then starts to come down. As it falls you can make out roughly where it should land, and you at once " proceed at the double " to the end of the Playground furthest away from its portable resting-place. It is a fine game, with just the right element of luck—sometimes the wind blows the bomb to your end—and one which encourages initiative and rapid power of decision, two qualities much sought after in military circles. As usual the Hun has not played fair, and this morning he started two Minnies going from different places and directed at opposite ends of the Playground. Luckily mine is now a roving commission, and I remembered that I had to examine bombs at the other end of the battalion sector. That's the Hun all over, never able to see that a game's a game.

The people over the way are Saxons and a peace-loving band. The other day at " stand to " in the morning we discovered that during the night they had put up a notice on the parapet of their trench. As it became light we were able to make it out. Here it is :

WE ARE SAXONS

YOU HAVE KILLED OUR MAJOR

HE WAS A PRUSSIAN

THANK YOU

They do love each other, don't they ?

To-night we are to be relieved—worse luck. We had hoped for a longer spell in the trenches. Now we have to go back to camp, and rest, and do early morning parade at 5.30 a.m. We have still another so-called camp now. It is situated in a field in dry weather, and in a lake in wet. To-night it is certain to rain. I'm glad that the first seven years of the war are going to be the worst.

Thy

THOMAS.

CAMP,

August 6th.

DEAR PHYLLIS,

These flies are a P-erfect P-est. Fly-papers are no good either. You place a fly-paper at the top of the tent pole and in five minutes it is covered to a depth of a quarter of an inch in glutinous flies which fall off on to your devoted head, where they become imbedded in your hair. Sticky flies are horrible things to comb out. Still it doesn't really matter now, for a real live general was round the other day and said that the war would end in November. And it wasn't the same general either who told one of the regular battalions that it would be over last November, or even the one that told us when we first came out that we were just in time to see the end of it.

To-day's *Daily Lie* was rather amusing. The *Daily Lie*, by the way, is the sheet of paper issued daily by the staff with news of what is happening on our own Divisional front, as well as little items of general interest culled from *Tit-Bits* and last Thursday's *Times*. It starts off with a long list of places from which German artillery have been observed to fire. It is so nice for you to know that the shells which are decimating your platoon are probably coming from the point O.15 d$7\frac{1}{2}$. $3\frac{1}{2}$. It makes it so homelike. The next paragraph is devoted to " Enemy Movements," and corresponds to the page of society news written by MR. TITTLE in the *Daily Tattle.* " This morning a German was observed opposite the bombing post at Q.18. a1.7. He was wearing a grey tunic with touches of red at the cuffs, and with a red and grey cap. He appeared to be unshaven." Such is a typical extract from this part of the rag. The next section is headed, " Casualties inflicted on the enemy," and goes somewhat in this style : " Last night an enemy working party was located putting out wire in front of their trenches at The Snout. Machine gun fire was directed at them and loud cries were heard. A whistle was blown (this is thought to be the signal for stretcher-bearers). This morning marks of blood could be made out on the parapet of the trench outside which the enemy was working." No obituary notice of this kind is ever complete without the reference to the whistle and the stretcher-bearers. It lends just that touch of realistic detail which is required. The concluding paragraph is entitled " Miscellaneous," and it is in this part that the gem of the season appeared to-day. It was a collection of extracts from the diary of a Hun captured at the crater. It read as follows :

June 3.　" Lieut. Reinaker is drunk.

June 7.　" Lieut. Reinaker is drunk again.

June 15.　" Once again Lieut. Reinaker is drunk.

June 21.　" To-day we attacked. As we advanced Lieut. Reinaker could be heard shouting ' *Vorwärts* ' from a dug-out in the support line.

July 15.　" Lieut. Reinaker has received the Iron Cross."

Not such a bad tale, was it ? Here's another which, as it happens, relates to the doings of one of our snipers. In the *Daily Lie* of the 21st there appeared the following :

" At R.34 b8.4. a dug-out has been observed by a sniper. On the door is a notice, Hauptmann Schmidt 213 Reg."

On the 23rd there appeared :

" A sniper claims to have hit the officer referred to in the *communiqué* of the 21st."

The sequel came on the 27th:

" With the aid of a powerful telescope a sniper was able to read some of the names on the crosses in the German graveyard at R.34 b9.7. On the newest-looking cross is the inscription HAUPTMANN SCHMIDT 213 Reg."

Evidently a bull.

You are sure to have read about the Germans retaking the crater from our successors there. On the night that it happened we were out on a digging fatigue, burying a cable I think it was, when the show started. We had just crossed the canal, and were getting to work, when the most awful din started, and the ground all round Hooge and Sanctuary Wood was lit up with flame—we afterwards found that it was the new instrument of kultur, the *Flamenwerfer*. Everywhere there seemed to be shells bursting, the crashing thunder of the crumps and the vicious moaning swish of the smaller guns. Then our guns—we were right in among them at the time—opened with a roar, which deafened our ears to all other sounds. We moved off to the right where things seemed a bit quieter, for we were out to work and not to be killed, and from the shelter of an embankment we watched. Lights of all colours were shooting up, red, green, yellow, blue, and white, and just in front of us was a continuous line of wicked red stabs of flame, about as high as the tops of the trees, the German barrage of shrapnel and gas shells. And all the time the heaviest of the shells were falling into Ypres, smashing and tearing down the few remaining buildings in the endeavour to keep off the ammunition and reinforcements coming up. It was a wonderful sight, far more wonderful than all the firework displays in the world put together, but so accustomed do you get to this sort of thing that as soon as the shelling quietened down a bit we started off on our very prosaic job and thought no more of the bombardment except perhaps to bless it for a little extra light to work by. Next morning we heard what had happened, and it made us pretty depressed to think that we had lost so many good lives in taking that place only for the Germans to retake it.

Now I'm waxing gloomy, so I'd better stop.

Your

THOMAS.

August 12th.

Back in camp again after a moderately peaceful tour in the trenches. This time we were on the banks of a canal, and in our spare moments could gaze upon masses of bulrushes and beautiful water-lilies. The more daring bathed in the lock until it was pointed out to them that to comply with trench orders they must wear their equipment and carry their rifles while so doing.

They've retaken the crater, as you must have seen. It was a brilliant affair, I believe. We like to think that we also helped in this, as while the attack was being made up at Hooge we were " demonstrating " down our part of the world, the idea being that Fritz would think we were about to go over the top and would divert half his guns from Hooge on to us. True heroism, eh ? At the same time as the bombardment started up north we began our little performance. Over our heads screeched salvos from an enthusiastic battery of very excited Belgians close behind. From our own trenches arose clouds (more or less) of trench mortar bombs, rifle grenades, catapult bombs, and what not, the while we cheered and issued orders to charge in our most stentorian tones. Did the Hun turn his guns on us ? He did. But not till the next day when all was quiet up Hooge way. Did the Huns in the trenches over the way shiver with fear and wait with palsied limbs for the attack which was doubtless to be launched? To be strictly truthful, Phyllis, they did not. From their trenches rose little columns of smoke, and wafted across by the breeze came the odour of fried bacon. They were cooking their breakfast! We could have sung the 'Ymn of 'Ate all right, I can tell you.

The only incident worth recording during our demonstration was a Harry Tate turn by myself on the latest pattern catapult. The corporal in charge of it came to me and told me that he couldn't quite understand the new release on it, and would I come and show them how it worked. I would. It takes three to work, two of whom disappear round the nearest traverse or protecting wall of sandbags, before the third looses it off. When it was, in my opinion, ready to fire, I sent the men under cover and lit the fuse. Five seconds after the fuze is lit the bomb explodes. Then I released the firing lever. Nothing happened, except that the bomb stayed quite still with the fuze burning merrily away. I had another shot, but without success, and stood there wondering what I should do. When the fuse had less than a second to burn I had a brain wave, and decided to leave for the corner instead of waiting to be blown forcibly to an unknown destination. Just as I disappeared round the corner the bomb went off, blowing the catapult out over the top of the trench, and tearing a hole in the last disappearing pleat of my kilt. As I was rounding the corner at full speed the C.O. was rounding it in more leisurely fashion from the opposite direction. I had the misfortune to knock

him over. After the excitement had died down someone suggested that it would have been simplest to
remove the bomb and throw it over the top of the parapet when I found it wouldn't go away. I do hate
people who tell you what you ought to have done,
don't you ?

As we came home from the trenches we passed
through the grounds of a château. Through the
most beautiful gardens we wended our way, and over
a delightful little moat, which must at one time have
been the home of many gold-fish. Through a hole in
the white walls of the building the setting sun was
shining, blood red, tinting the clouds of mist a delicate
pink. It was so beautiful there, and everything was
so quiet and peaceful that I grew quite sentimental.
Turning to the man with whom I was walking, I
whispered with reverential awe, " Doesn't this remind
you of the good old days before the war ? " " Yes,"
he replied, but there was no awe in his voice, " it does.
But how did you know that this place belonged to the
man who makes Three Star Brandy ? " Not quite
what I meant.

We seem to have been annoying the Hun with our
old gas-pipes, because on a prisoner taken the other
day was a circular stating that seven hundred and
fifty marks would be paid to any soldier capturing a
British trench mortar. As they can't cost more than
about ten bob each, we are on the look out for a friendly
Hun across the way who would be willing to take half
shares in the profit with us, for there would be

about £30 on each, notwithstanding the fall in the mark.

Went into Poperinghe for tea yesterday. It was the first time that I had ridden upon a horse since I was a very wee kid, and the result was simply stupendous. The transport sergeant in his humorous little way provided me with the only real horse which the battalion possesses. The others are of the usual officer's (infantry) charger type, pack ponies which are no longer strong enough to carry two boxes of ammunition. But mine was in very truth a charger. It was a hunter before the war, and had not had any exercise for three or four weeks. On the way out it was not so bad, as no horse seems too keen to gallop away from home. When we reached Pop I was still on top, very sore all over and five minutes ahead of the others. The joy of being in a town again was too much for us, and we bought heaps of rubbish for which we had no use, just for the love of buying. We had tea in a café presided over by a twelve-year-old maiden, who spoke English passing well, and rejoiced in the name of Ginger. After tea we went to a café and had lemon squash. It is curious how closely Belgian lemon squash resembles the British whisky and soda. Then we set off home. I mounted, with aid. The man who was holding on to the reins let go, and my steed started like a flash of lightning without even turning round to ask "where to." Through the streets of Pop we flashed, scattering traffic right and left. One brigadier, whom I, or my charger to be accurate, caused to leave the middle of the road in a great hurry, shouted out to me to stop. That was impossible, but I tried to salute him with my left hand—my right was fully engaged hanging on to the saddle ; but the salute must have resembled a waved farewell more than anything else. Once out of the town, my brute took it into his head to go across country in a bee-line for the camp. No hedge or ditch was too high for us, and we arrived home twenty-five minutes ahead of the rest of the party. It was rather pleasing once I had quite determined that I should not get home alive, and the way in which I landed on some portion of that animal's back after every jump was simply miraculous. To-day I don't seem to have any skin left upon certain parts of my body, and my bones rattle when I walk. Next time I am going to insist on a charger of the superannuated pack pony description.

Cheero.

Your aching

THOMAS.

CAMP,

August 22nd.

DEAR PHIL,

I nearly arrived back in camp last night a corpse. 'Twas thus : One of the communication trenches, leading up to the firing line where we were, starts on the safe side of a small rise in the ground which enables you to walk right up to it unseen. It is called " Pear Tree Walk " from a fruit tree of some description that grows at the bottom end of it, and on its higher branches are a few pears or apples or something of that sort. Yesterday, just before we were relieved, I decided to climb up this tree and discover whether the fruit was ripe, as if it was it seemed a pity to waste it on the unappreciative palates of the incoming battalion. Accordingly I scrambled up and was just reaching for the nearest pear when bullets started to whistle all round me. Then it struck me that though the bottom of the tree was out of sight the top was in full view, and I lost no time in trying to come down, but in my haste I let my kilt catch in a branch and found myself suspended in mid-air, an 800 yards target to the Hun. I yelled for help, and the signal officer came round the corner. He looked at me for a moment and then dashed off for help, or so I imagined. The bullets were whistling all round me, and I was making frantic efforts to escape, but nothing I could do was of any use, and it was with a sigh of relief that I saw the signalling officer coming back at the double. Then I noticed to my dismay that he was alone, but just as he arrived under the tree the branch gave way and down I came on top of him. When he had re-covered sufficient breath to swear, " You fool," he gasped, " couldn't you have managed to stay up there another minute after I had run all the way to battalion headquarters and back for my camera ? "

The officers' lines in this camp would give pleasure

to the wildest Futurist. Nowhere have I seen such a riot of colour before. The first tent, the C.O.'s, is a mass of clashing patches, red, green, yellow, blue, brown, and other less easily determined shades. Next door lives the *padre*, and his domicile has been soaked in soot which gives it a funereal appearance. The third tent is the abode of the second in command and the adjutant, an orderly fellow who has had it done in tasteful blue and red check. The quartermaster, transport officer, and interpreter share number four, which has been painted red, white, and blue, in rings, out of compliment to our gallant ally. The four company commanders, having minds above any mere foolery, have daubed theirs with mud pure and simple, which gives it an earthy appearance—and smell. A, B, C, and D Companies' subs, each in his own little palace, have worked out schemes of their own. A Company's, for sheer brilliance of colouring, compares favourably with Turner's most gorgeous sunsets. B Company's is Early Renaissance, and C's Rembrandtesque. D Company have turned theirs into a wigwam in which rather doubtful figures in brown and blue walk unnaturally upon a background of verdant green. Our tent—the specialist officers are us—is up to the present unadorned save for a sprig of hawthorn which we have pinned over the entrance in order to comply with D.R.O. 765804 or thereabouts, which states that all tents must be disguised either by painting or by covering with green-stuff. We have not yet decided what to do with the unblemished whiteness of ours. Some people have been heard to say that we are too lazy and too fond of joy rides to Pop. We treat all such remarks with despisery. The amusing part about the tents is that before they came up from the base they were all painted earth brown on one side, but the gem who painted them had painted the inside !

It is most comforting to sit outside your tent these hot evenings and watch the men go by on their journey up to the trenches. To sit there delightfully cool and watch others marching along in a semi-liquid condition is very satisfying, even though you know that in a day or two it will be your turn. The old regular battalions and the Territorials who have now been out a long time take it very easy on the way up, but some of the latest arrivals have not yet learned their lesson and they swing past, endeavouring to keep step with the brass band at their head, an amusing mixture of swank and sweat, or to put it rather more politely, pomp and perspiration. They'll learn, however, and though we may laugh at them now and then we know that they are all right. You've no idea how vastly superior a person who's been out here three months thinks himself to the latest addition to the B.E.F.

I have just patented a new method of killing flies. It's all done by kindness. First tighten up the guide ropes of the tent until the canvas is as taut as a drum. Take in one hand a stick, and in the other a fly-paper, grasping it gently but firmly with the thumb and forefinger. Advance warily to the side of the tent upon which the unsuspecting pest will be snoozing, and bring the fly paper stealthily to within two or three inches of your prey. Then deal the tent a resounding thwack—whatever that is—with your stick. The rebound of the tent will project the fly automatically in the direction of the fly-paper against which it will subsequently impinge and to which it will eventually adhere. If it does not do so money will be returned promptly. Never known to fail. Penalty for improper use not to exceed five miles per hour, etc., etc.

More news from the *Daily Lie*. A letter found on a prisoner describes the crater in words of glowing endearment which are pleasing for us, who did not have too happy a time there ourselves, to read. " This once so peaceful spot," he writes, " has now for itself the name Hell Fire earned."

The Hun has been amusing himself lately by shelling the farms all round us. It is a pretty sight. So far he hasn't had a go at our own particular one, but we are daily living in the expectation, if not in the hope, of seeing it made into a pretty sight also.

Have just heard that we are bound for our old and warm haunts. That's the worst of being in a division so noted for its way of clinging to insalubrious salients. Whenever there's likely to be any Hate coming off we're sent up to absorb it. Still I suppose we ought to be only too proud of the honour.

Your
THOMAS.

SANCTUARY WOOD

CHAPTER IV

SANCTUARY WOOD

THE APPENDIX,

September 2nd.

MY DEAR PHYLLIS,

Don't get worried over the address, as the Appendix is only the name of a trench. Into it this morning fell a round body of about the same size and shape as a bomb. We all scooted round the corner for a few seconds, and then as there was no explosion we went back, to discover an old jam tin lying on the trench boards. We picked it up and found inside a message. " Dear Jocks, I have a wife in Falkirk. What would happen if I came over to you to-night ? " " There would be another widow in Falkirk " was the reply.

Our one chair became a casualty this morning. About nine a small and wiry individual came to our dug-out and said that he was the 2 inch. By this he meant that he was the *deus ex machina* of the local two inch trench mortar. We invited him in and sat him down upon the chair, which, though dilapidated, bore his weight. We passed him the whisky and he helped himself to a very modest tot, a two inch one. Then he went out in quest of machine gun emplacements to strafe and we were left alone for about five minutes, after which a middle-sized gentleman poked in his head and asked for the telephone dug-out. Him we invited in. He explained that he was the 4.7 inch and took a peg in proportion. When he sat down in the chair it began to creak. He was followed by the F.O.O. of the siege battery, who introduced himself as the 6 inch. Him we gave a 6-inch drink as he sat on the swaying chair, for he was somewhat cumbersome. Half an hour later the 9.2 showed himself at the door, through which he was pushed by his linesman. He was enormous. When the chair had collapsed under him, we fetched out the bottle and he drank his 9.2 drink upon the floor. He left with thanks and an intimation that the 15-inch man might soon be along. We looked at each other, then at the chair. It was past repair, but we set it up true to life and waited for the 15-incher to come and sit on it. We felt that we deserved something at the hands of the artillery. Then we looked at the whisky bottle, now sadly depleted. Without a word the machine gun officer stretched forth his hand and took it. From his pocket he produced the stub of a pencil. " Paraffin Oil," he wrote in large letters across the label. " A lie," he remarked to me, " is an abomination in the sight of the Lord, but a very present help in time of trouble." Whereupon the 15-incher did turn up. He was five foot three high, couldn't possibly stop for a moment and wouldn't have a drink thanks as he was a tee-totaller. Not much luck in this life, is there ?

Artillery officers are fairly swarming round us these days. They come up with a telephone and batter the German trenches, and occasionally our own. But to us it looks as if the enemy's trenches are still there, and certainly their barbed wire is. Ough, that barbed wire, and the ground in between them and us is becoming more broken up than ever, and each day sees several more trees down, and altogether things look cheerful for us when—— Oh, all right, Mr. Censor, I was only going to say when we go out to pick mushrooms in " No Man's Land."

That's about all there is to report to-day,

So farewell.

Your

Thomas.

In Bed,

September 16th.

Fair One,

I am in luck to-night. From time to time when we are back in camp we have guest nights. A guest night is a function at which the C.O. and senior major talk to the guests for several hours while you, at the other end of the table, try not to fall fast asleep. To-night is a guest night, and the brigadier and the brigade major are here. It is no doubt very thrilling for the

C.O. to have a real live brigadier to bore for a whole evening, and the adjutant has hopes that if he puts enough port into the brigade major he will forget that " A reply hás not yet been received to my B.M. 537 of the 14th ult." But for me the prospect was one of sheer ennui, and so I welcomed the little incident which has sent me to bed with outstretched arms. Just behind my tent, and between it and my batman's bivvy, there lies a little pond of slimy green water of the kind which is so frequently to be seen in dear little Belgium. Desiring to speak to my servant, and not thinking what I was doing, I walked into this pond, and trying to get out of it in the dark tripped, and fell right in over my shoulders. I issued green and smelly, and had to retire to bed while my only suit (we are travelling pretty light just now for various reasons) was hung up on the line. So here I am, lying comfortably in my flea-bag writing to you while my servant brings me in lordly dishes from the mess. I have just suggested to him that where brigadiers are, there also is champagne. He has taken a tin mug and gone off in search.

We've been playing cricket just lately, some game I can tell you with a pitch that would disgrace the outfield of any country ground, and demon bowlers galore. A kilt isn't much protection to your shins either. We are thinking of laying down cement tennis courts if the war goes on much longer, as we have managed to coax two barrels of cement out of the D.A.D.O.S. on the excuse of making an ablution place.

Up Hooge way we could get a splendid links, except for the greens. Just think what a topping hole could be made out of the crater for instance, and there's no shortage of bunkers. And now I'm going to play auction, as the other inmates of my tent have escaped from the mess.

Good night.

THOMAS.

CAMP,

September 22nd.

DEAR PHIL,

Who do you think we've had here to-day? Sssssssh. And why did he come? Sssssssh. And what did he say? Sssssssh.

You want to know what I and the bombers do to amuse ourselves when we are in camp. Herewith please find a sample. Rising at 6.30 a.m. we run and march rapidly to the mill and back. On our return breakfast awaits us. After breakfast rifles are inspected and any sinners are brought before the judgment-seat. At about 9.30 we push off to some practice trenches a mile or two away, and when we are well out of sight of C.O.'s and brigade Staffs we play about for a few hours. This morning, for example, we captured a section of trenches with terrific realism. Everything was done just as if it was the real thing. For instance, one lance-corporal was told off to act as the German artillery. Whenever that worthy shouted out the

name of any bomber the individual named had to fall
down and be a casualty. He was rather too ready
with his salvos, and in about a minute and a half
everybody was down and out, and so we had to start
all again, but this time I took on the roll of honour.
Before starting I gave out that when I blew the whistle
once every man whose name began with an A was to
consider himself a corpse. The next time the B's.
And so on. It was very hot. I blew the whistle.
Every man's name seemed to begin with an A, for
they all fell down, after which we had to start again,
but this time with a deathless army. The attack succeeded, bombing parties advanced up the C.T.'s
bombing as they went, carrying parties brought up
reserves of bombs, blocking parties began their work,
and everything was going smoothly when my second
in command walked up and started to give orders.
As he had been left in reserve with orders not to come
up until sent for, I asked him what he was doing.
" Oh," said he, " word came back that you had fallen
into a shell hole and been drowned, so of course I came
up to take command," which I imagine was their way
of letting me know that they had heard of my soaking
in the pond the other night. By this time there were
no more worlds to conquer as we had come to the end
of the trenches, so I gathered my flock around me, let
them sit down and smoke, and started to lecture them
on " the origin of bombs and how they first came to
be used in trench warfare." Before long a gentle
droning sound rose from them, the heat and my voice

had done the trick. Together we slept. At noon I roused them and did a little close-order drill, which is not their strong point. Then we marched home singing, and fed. In the afternoon we threw live bombs. Not a very strenuous sort of day, was it ? but there seems just a chance that the end of the week will find them with plenty of work on their hands. If it does, so much the better. We're getting fed up with the waiting. Here's to the day !

Your
THOMAS.

NO NEARER TO BERLIN,

September 27th.

OH, PHYLLIS,

I saw six men and a juvenile N.C.O. coming along the road. As they passed I hailed the leader. " Why aren't you marching home with your platoon ? " " Platoon, sir ? " he answered. " This is D Company."

There was one sight on that awful day which I shall never forget. Stumbling backwards down the trench came a very scared Tommy. It was evidently his first show, and his bayonet was not a quarter of an inch off the breast of the first of a string of about twenty Hun prisoners. He was quite as terrified of them as they seemed to be of him. He was going very slowly. At the other end of the procession was a brawny Highlander, enjoying himself no end, and constantly reminding the last of the bunch that time was valuable. Hun Number One wasn't wanting to get on fast. The progress of the bayonet in front of him was too slow. Hun Number Twenty was in no end of a hurry. The consequence was that the twenty of them were squeezed up into about seven yards of trench, and were becoming more condensed every minute.

Poor X, he was killed later on in the day, had not been with us for long. He was all out for strafing the Hun. The first one he saw he was going to do this and that to, and say that and this, and in fact the feathers were going to fly some. Round the corner came a draggled grey figure, his right sleeve in tatters and blood dripping down his arm. We turned to X and waited for the fireworks. "Er-er," he began, "er-er-good morning, better have a drink out of this," and he pressed his flask to the lips of the astonished, but obedient, Teuton, who, I am sure, thought he was being poisoned.

To-day and yesterday generals have been rolling up, patting us on the back, and telling us how our show has helped the bigger ones down South, which is all very well, but there's not much to show for it. Can't write any more just now.

Your
Thomas.

Oh, if only we'd had more shells and men to back us up.

BACK IN THE WOOD,

October 7th.

DEAR PHYLLIS,

Here we are back again on the scene of the attack of the 25th. And what a poor washed-out remnant we are too. One company—eighty strong—consists of the remnants of B, C, and D Companies, under the guidance of the signalling sergeant. The bombers are about thirty strong, but they include many recruits from the companies. Since the show, we have been so hard up for them that instead of giving a long training to the would-be anarchists we pick out likely looking men from the companies, draw them up in line, and tell them that they are bombers. And bombers they have to become forthwith.

We have been having a perfectly ghastly time this last fortnight. After we got back to camp from the show there were rumours of a month's rest. We rejoiced, forgetting that last time that that rumour raised its grisly head we did almost a month running in the front line. It looks as if history was going to repeat itself this time, as we are now in our thirteenth day.

On the night after the 25th we went off to bed pretty early, as we weren't feeling very fit. It must have been just about nine o'clock when we blew out the candle, and hardly had we done so before a terrific bombardo started. We looked out of the door of the hut and saw that it was coming from the old place. Louder and louder it grew, and we looked at each other in dismay, for we thought that we should be turned out of bed and sent up. For half an hour we lay and listened, trying to detect the hum of a motor-bike from out the roar of the guns. Suddenly the expected sound came, and I for one lay shivering, waiting for some one to dash in and tell us to get ready to move. The door flung open, and there stood a dispatch rider. " Bombing officer here ? " he cried in a loud voice. Evidently the bombers were wanted up there. My heart sank still further into my boots, but I just managed to answer that I was. " Urgent message for you, sir," and he handed me a pink slip. With trembling hands I lit a candle and unfolded the paper. At that moment I would have exchanged places with anybody in the world. But as I read there came to me a great sensation of relief. " Detail at once," ran the chit, " two bombers to attend the Divisional Grenade School." We aren't heroes exactly, are we ?

In the morning we heard the explanation of the trouble, and it goes to show you how high-strung and panicky both sides become after a few days of fighting like this. Two men of an English regiment had gone out over the parapet to bring in a wounded man who could be heard crying for help outside. By the light o: a flare the Germans had seen figures approaching their trench, and taking alarm they had started to hurl salvos of grenades out into their own wire. The men in our trenches, being a bit windy and hearing the awful din, thought the Hun was attacking, and started off rapid fire, although if they had thought about it a bit they would have realised that people who were bombing their own wire couldn't be attacking. This persuaded the Hun that we were on the way over (through our own rapid fire, mark you), and he sent out the S.O.S. to his artillery. Our artillery took the hint from theirs and in a minute a first-class attack was going on without anybody wanting to attack. It took them almost an hour to find out that the whole thing was a gigantic "wind up." At the time that the bombardment started, our transport had just arrived behind the supports, and rations were being off loaded. Thinking that the Hun was upon them, the transport turned tail and galloped off at full tilt, as was only right for them to do. It would have been stupid for them to stay and get captured with all their horses and limbers. At the same time the German transport, which was also close to the trenches, deeming discretion the better part of valour, made a bee-line for distant Roulers. The men who were in the trenches at the time say that they heard the noise of the retreating transport above the roar of the guns, and I can well believe it, as in the ordinary way, coming up at a walk, you can often hear the German rations being brought up to some spot or another behind their trenches.

The next alarm wasn't a false one. It came at 3.30 in the morning, the first winter morning of the year. The adjutant rushed in and told us we had to be off in half an hour, and as the guns were going hard in the same old place we didn't need to be told where we were bound. Cold, cheerless, and breakfastless, we started off, and surely the pipes have never sounded more mournful than they did as we plodded on through the slush, getting wetter every moment. Just out of Ypres we halted and lay down in a field to wait for bombs. The Germans were shelling our batteries near the moat, and as the shells exploded in it great columns of water rose high above the trees, glistening in the sun, which at that moment started to shine through the clouds. At any other time this would have been a sight worth watching, but we felt too miserable. After an hour of waiting, our travelling kitchens came up with steaming tea and bacon, and we were soon feeling fitter. Hardly had we finished than the bombs arrived, and every man was given twenty to take up with him, in addition to the whole of his worldly goods. Then came a four-mile cross-country trek, sometimes with communication trenches knee-deep in mud to help (?) you along, and sometimes across the open. Meanwhile Fritz was having no end of a good time shelling us, directed by an accursed sausage up in the air which could spot our every movement. Ooo! It is a cheerful feeling to hear a shell falling, falling, falling, always nearer to you, and to know that you are stuck fast in the mud and carrying enough explosives on your back to blow up the House of Lords. We arrived about three in the afternoon, absolutely done up, to find that we were just too late to take part in a counter attack on a part of our old position, which the Hun had mined. However, we had to get back as fast as we could to the village of the church with the organ, and find what cover we could there, which was none, while the bombardment and the counter barrages were on. At dusk we were called out again to do another counter attack, but before we got to the trenches it was countermanded and we were sent to chew the cud in a very wet and cold communication trench. About midnight we heard our fate, which was to go up to the wood in support. A guide came along to take us to the dug-outs. Guides are of two kinds—those who admit that they don't know the way, and those who don't admit it. Ours was the latter class. As he had ascended rapidly in the mine earlier on in the day you couldn't expect him to be very bright, in fact it was a tribute to the hardness of his head that he was still alive. He led us over all the wettest places, through the thickest brushwood, among the most formidable of our support line wire entanglements, over the widest and slipperiest trenches, and finally turned round and asked me which way I thought we ought to go now. If I had still had enough energy I am sure that I would have killed him. It would have been for the best. Eventually we arrived at the dug-outs and found that the bombardment of the last few days had reduced them to ruins, which had been rendered more picturesque, but less desirable, by several inches of water. None of us slept that night, we were too tired. We just lay and felt the water in our boots turning into ice. Next day we relieved the poor chaps who had had it so badly in the neck. Their regimental motto is "Die Hard," but they've been finding it pretty easy just lately. So here we are, a noble band no doubt, but most of us with flue or worse. I've never seen a more done up looking lot, and I never want to.

Good-bye.

Your

THOMAS.

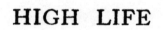

HIGH LIFE

CHAPTER V

HIGH LIFE

BRIGADE HEADQUARTERS,

October 18th.

DEAR MADAM,

Please note change in address.

I am on the brigade Staff and have hot water to wash in.

Yesterday came the news that I was indispensable to the higher command. In other words I was the only bombing officer left in the brigade, and they wanted some one to do that sort of thing. Hence proposition, as we used to say. When the wire came I sank down in a swoon. In the words of Sydney Carton, " This is a far better rest that I go to than I have ever known," I gasped, but I wasn't right, as there seems to be quite a lot of work to do. It appears that you do work on the Staff after all. Of course it isn't considered correct to be caught out working, and that's why, when you enter the brigade office, you may find the brigade major peppering the Staff captain with paper balls. It's only done so that you may think that they don't work. If it was once discovered that the Staff worked as hard as other people, the chief grouse of the British Army would be taken away, and it is well known that the British Army without a grouse would be as heartbroken as an A.S.C. (Motor Transport) officer without spurs.

The message said that I was to report to the brigadier at 8 a.m. Therefore at 8 a.m. exactly I knocked at the door of his dug-out. I don't think I should have taken the message so literally, as after a pause the door opened a few inches and portions of the general appeared, clad in an eye-glass and a selection of intimate underclothing of a woolly character. He looked at me as if I had come for the rent, and so I disappeared. Isn't it a terrible war ?

My dug-out here is of the very selectest. A 4.5-inch crump landed on top of it yesterday and exploded, but nothing untoward happened. In fact it is rather enjoyable to hear the shells pattering on your roof. It reminds one of home in April.

Cheero.

Your

THOMAS.

P.S.—They don't allow me red tabs, which is a cruel shame, as leave ought to be along again soon.

THE GAS WORKS,
A WEE TOWN,
FRANCE,

November 1st.

DEAR GIRL,

Here are we once more upon French soil, bless it. Enough of Belgium for many a day. " Soon, soon, to faithful warriors comes a rest," as the hymn says, which means that after a year of trial and tribulation our poor old emaciated division, consolidation contractors, frightfulness frustrators, salient saviours, etc., etc., has been pulled out for a rest, though some say that we are only out for a day or two on our way down to Loos, and others, more daring still, prophesy Mesopotamia at an early date. However, I 'opes not, as we are very comfy here. On fine days I ride round and see the people with whom I have business, and on wet days I wire for them to come and see me. This is the life.

I am billeted in a wine shop, and have a nice bed with white sheets. The only crab is that in these parts the bed-clothing consists of sheets and a *duvet*, an enormous sort of pillow which takes the place of blankets, counterpane, and all. The result is that after you get into bed you are beautifully warm for a short time, but then you fall asleep and move about a quarter of an inch, whereupon off slides the *duvet*, and you wake up a block of ice. The old gentleman who keeps the place means well, but his idea of French and mine vary considerably. Thus when I tried to get a second latchkey for the use of my servant he was completely nonplussed for some time, but it eventually dawned upon him that I was not an " *officier* " after all but my own servant, which wasn't quite what I started out to prove.

No, I am not a brigade major.

Our mess is in the gas works, and we are waited on by a fair young thing who is much enamoured of my kilt. While she waits she beguiles us with stories of the officers who have been billeted on them before us. Of one, a Canadian, she was especially proud.

A cinema has been started in one of the barns here, and we are going to see Charlie Chaplin, who seems to be all the rage now, so I shall have to stop.

Your
THOMAS.

THE GAS WORKS,

November 10th.

DEAR PHYLLIS,

Our rest continues satisfactorily, and despite all sorts of wild rumours we look as if we are here for several weeks. But don't get into your head that a rest, as understood by the Army, is the same thing as a rest cure. It is a period spent in feverish activity, trying to get people to look like soldiers again. Of course it's very nice to be well out of the way of Skinny Liz, the eight-point two, and Silent Sue, the naval gun, but the further away from them you get the nearer do you approach to the home of the Red Hats, and if you allow the men two minutes' real repose along comes some old fellow and asks you why the ahem, ahem, you think that you have been withdrawn to the training area.

The brigade is but the shadow of its former self. Two of the regular battalions and my own 'umble Terrier one were given to a K brigade in exchange for two of their battalions and a Territorial battalion up from the L. of C., and now still a third has gone and has been succeeded by one of the unfortunate lot who made a fleeting appearance at the battle of Loos. Poor chaps, they had a bit of a doing before they had shaken down, and just at present are rather a rabble. They are officered by a major and thirty war babies, war babies being the technical turn for freshly arrived subs. They'll settle down no doubt. The other two K battalions came out since Loos and are green as green can be, but full of enthusiasm and a desire to hunt the Hun. We ought to have quite a good army by next spring.

We went to see Charlie Chaplin and were much entertained, although the machine did break down for half an hour or so. The audience was a mixed one. At the front was a rather noisy section of the divisional salvage squad. At the back was a major-general complete with red-tabbed following. In between, every sort of soldier, loud-voiced Cockney and stolid farm hand from Suffolk, brawny Highlander and wiry lowland Scot, gunner and A.S.C. driver, sapper and trooper, with every here and there a leather-capped Australian M.T. man and steel-helmeted, blue-clad *poilu*. And when Charles, with his usual deadly aim, registered a direct hit with a brick upon the face of the policeman, who laughed most, the major-general or the bugler boy in the second row ? And when the light failed and the pianist struck up popular tunes, was that the voice of his chief of staff which you could hear among the rest singing, " Hullo, hullo, and who's your lady friend ? " or was it just my imagination ?

You've no idea what a busy life generals have to live out here. I am seeing a bit of it now, and you can take it from me that they are up and about as much as any man under them. From dawn to midnight one thing or another has to be done, and in the trenches, when they are round some part of their line every day, no rest is theirs. Some generals, though, don't agree with constant paddling round the firing line, which they say is not the proper place for them. Perhaps they're right, but the British working man, Tommy I mean, dearly loves to have his own little bit of gold braid round to see him, and the further forward the more he likes it. In connection with which I heard this little tale. One day, a being with much red on his hat strolled round the bombing posts. After he had left one bomber turned to his companion :

" Say ? "

" Wal."

" Who's that ? "

" The brigadier."

" That so ? "

" Sure."

" Is peace declared ? "

Did you hear of John's engagement ? It's absurd the people who are getting that way now, isn't it ? Why, he's no older than I am, and she's younger still. What fools these mortals be. You don't find me succumbing to anybody before the end of the war.

Cheero.

THOMAS.

The Staff captain has just told me that I'm for leave the day after to-morrow, so look out for me in a few days.—T.

THE GAS WORKS,

November 21st.

DARLING,

I can hardly believe that we are really en———

(Circumstances over which the author had little or no control have caused much to enter into this and subsequent letters which would be of no interest to the reader. Large portions of, and in some cases entire,

letters have therefore been omitted without detriment
to the narrative.)

We had rather a rotten journey again, as it was
very cold and several things went wrong. When
we did get in, about 11 p.m., we found that there
was no train for us, as of course it had started
from Boulogne hours ago, and had long since passed
through Calais. We were told that the next one
would soon arrive, and so we waited on the bleak
platform and saw the dawn before we did get off.
At railhead we found a bus waiting to take us here,
but it had been standing still for most of the night and
like ourselves was suffering from a cold inside. The
engine wouldn't start, and so we had to push it downhill for a good hundred yards before faint gurglings
from the bonnet gave promise of better things to come.
On the drive home I felt very drowsy, and fell into a
doze, from which I wakened in the act of putting my
arm round the waist of my next door neighbour, the
colonel of a pioneer battalion. I suppose that it was
the purr of the engine awakening in me the habits of
the past week.

Have just come from a Court of Enquiry. The way
that justice is dispensed in the army is wonderful.
Imagine the private parlour of a small French *estaminet*
cleared for action, the tile floor covered with sawdust
and a bright fire burning in the grate (thank the Lord
we are out of the land of stoves). In the centre of the
room a table with three chairs at the fire end of it, and
in front of them piles of blotting-paper, foolscap, pens

(but no ink), and a collection of books, foremost among which is the red-covered *Manual of Military Law*. So much for the setting of the stage. Now for the players. Punctual to the recognised time for starting these shows, half an hour late that is, enters Second Lieut. Dash, the junior of the three members of the Court. A few minutes later he is followed by the other two, Lieutenant Asterisk and Captain Blank, the President. They sit down on the chairs, Captain Blank in the centre, Lieutenant A. on the right, and Second Lieut. Dash on the left. The President lights a cigarette and offers his confrères his case, from which they also extract smokes. " Have you the foggiest idea what it's all about ? " he asks. The reply is an emphatic negative. They look through the papers in front of them, and the bunch with the requisite information is discovered. The President picks it up and glances through it. " Seems a good bit of it, doesn't there ? " They plod through the pile of documents. At last they have finished. " Better get a move on now," says the President. " How do you begin ? " Asterisk has been on a Court quite recently and remembers, or thinks he does, the wording of it. Dash takes one of the many sheets of paper and fishes an indelible pencil out of his pocket. " Fire ahead," he grunts, and writes to Asterisk's dictation.

" Proceedings of a Court of Enquiry assembled by order of Brigadier-General A. Bhoy at . . .—or should that come before the ' enquire into '—anyhow, leave it at that—. . . got that down, good !

" The Court, having assembled, proceed to take evidence."

" Finished," says the writer. " Shall I tell the sergeant to call in the first witness ? "

He does so.

From outside comes a roar, " Private Sloper, 'SHUN ! Ri'turn, quickmarchlefwheelriturnalt," and the first witness is manœuvred in. He stands in front of the table looking very sheepish, and out of sheer embarrassment starts to scratch his head.

" Stantenshun, Private Sloper," in stentorian tones from the sergeant.

" What is your name and number ? " asks the President, and when this has been given, " Well, what have you to say ? "

The oracle speaks. " I was acoming down the road from Sally Farm it might 'ave been Tuesday, sir, when I sees 'im——"

" See who ? "

" 'Im 'oo's outside, sir."

" He means Private Fowler, sir."

" I sees Privit Fowler comin' out of the 'ennouse. I ses to 'im ses I, ' 'Ullo Bill, 'ave you seen Charlie lately ? ' ' No,' ses 'e, ' I carntsaysIave.' ' Wot, not seen old Charlie ? ' ses I. ' Why 'e was askin' me for you las'night. Then 'e turns round to me, 'e does, and ses, ' Wotdyerthink of the beer 'ere, Tom.' ' Not much,' ses I, ' but the vinnblangs alrite.' "

" Half a second, Private Sloper. Did you see Private Fowler carrying any hens with him or not ? "

" Well, sir, I notices as 'ow 'e 'ad somethink under 'is tewnic, so I asks 'im, ' Wot the 'ell 'ave yer got there ? ' and 'e ses to me, ' Wot the 'ell's that gotter do with you ? ' ' You've been pinchin' 'ens,' ses I, ' I can see them under your tewnic.' ' 'Aven't I told yer ter mind yer own bloo——' "

" You haven't answered my question, Private Sloper. Did you or did you not see him taking away some hens ? "

" Yessir, an' I ses to 'im—— "

" That's enough. And had he his rifle with him ? "

" Yessir, an' I ses to 'im, ' Wot in the 'ell——' "

" That's enough. Have you got all that down, Mr. Dash ? "

" I was hardly able to keep up, sir."

" Well, write this down. I saw Private Fowler at four o'clock on the afternoon of the 17th November. He was coming out of La Ferme Salle and was carrying his rifle. Several hens were secreted underneath his tunic. That right, Private Sloper ? Right then, sign it," and the abridged version of his evidence is passed over to him.

His signature duly made, he retires, manœuvred out in the same way as he was manœuvred in. Outside he can be heard carrying on with his explanation of what he said to him, and what him said to he.

" Second witness," calls out the President, and from the outside comes the sergeant's voice, " Corporal Biggs, 'SHUN ! Ri'turn, quickmarchlefwheelriturnalt."

Corporal Biggs is no end of a fellow and gives a

terrific salute. He evidently knows what is expected of him, for, placing his head on one side and staring steadfastly two foot six above the head of the President, he starts at a terrific rate. "Sir-on-the-afternoon-of-the-17th-hinstant-at-about-four-p-hem-I-was-proceedin'-in-a-westerly-direction——"

"Half a moment, Corporal Biggs. Would you mind giving us your number and regiment? Right. You were passing the farm when you saw Private Fowler."

"Yessir. I saw him hissuing from the hentrance, equipped with his rifle. Underneath his jacket I noticed a suscipious procumference which hon hinvestigation proved to be three hens. Blood was dripping from newly formed hincisions, which, if my opinion be requested, were caused by bullets from a rifle or other such-like harticle. As he was unable to give any satisfactory explanation of how he came to be in possession of the aforesaid hens, I took charge of same and reported the matter to my platoon commander."

"Thank you, corporal. Very clearly put indeed. Please sign this, and do you mind telling me if you have ever been a policeman? I thought so. Next witness, please, sergeant."

The next witness is the owner of the hens. He is accompanied by the interpreter. After five minutes of the most frenzied word storm the interpreter speaks.

"Sir, zis is ze farmair to which ze chickens did

belong. 'E ses zat zey vas prize hens and zat they cost him fifty francs each one. But I do not sink that 'e the truth tells. If you like I vill ze birds fetch."

He brings them in, and they prove to be notable only for their skinniness. The owner is told that he will be repaid a fair price, and departs unhappy. The hens remain before the Court, lying on the table.

The final witness is Private Fowler. He comes in looking very sulky, and forgets to salute. Under the circumstances he can hardly help admitting that he had something to do with the lamentable end of the hens, but he tells a long and complicated tale of how he was trying a cartridge into his rifle, "just to see if it fitted," when the rifle went off by itself and the bullet went through all three hens. When found with the hens he was going in search of the farmer to compensate him. When he has finished the President looks at him.

"Are you going to stick to that tale, Private Fowler?"

"Yessir, it's the truth I'm telling."

"Certain? . . . I should think of something better if I were you. . . . Or what about telling the truth? . . . It is the truth. . . . Oh, all right, if you're going to put your money on it, come and sign." And as the man goes out, "Isn't it extraordinary what bad liars some people are?"

For a minute the case is discussed, and then, "The

Court, having considered the evidence, is of opinion that the three hens were shot by Private Fowler."

" Thank the Lord that's over," from Captain Blank. " But what about the hens ? "

From the *estaminet* slunk the three members of the Court. Each carried something shapeless wrapped up in a large sheet of blotting-paper.

And now the thing has been sent back to us to be done all over again as it was not in duplicate. How are we going to get the irate French farmer to identify the hens ?

There are signs of lunch, so farewell.

More than ever

Your

THOMAS.

BACK IN BELGIUM,

November 30th.

DARLING,

. . . . . .

Once more we " are in the midst of foes," and still in the Salient, bad cess to it. But we are further down this time and in what should prove a more peaceful spot. We are sharing trenches and rest camps with another brigade, and at present we are out and they are in. Brigade headquarters are four huts in a sea of mud, and the battalions are also imbedded more or less firmly in the same mixture. Our mess is a small

hut raised several feet off the mud by stakes. The
rain comes in through the roof, and the wind enters
by way of the floor, the windows, and the stove-pipe.
Apart from this it is a nice room, and the last occupants
have left us two copies of *La Vie Parisienne* and a
sheaf of *War Cry's*, the official journal of the Salvation
Army. The bedroom suite is some way off and across
an almost impassable road. Here we each have our
own little cubicle, and the walls are papered with
strips of red and blue stuff spangled with golden stars.
The whole edifice nearly went West last night when
one of the servants lit such a fire in the improvised
stove that the tin chimney became red-hot and set
one of the walls on fire. Luckily it was raining so hard
that the fire soon went out, but there is a large hole
burnt in the wall and many draughts enter therein
when you are dressing.

The terrors of war don't seem to be properly understood by the people in the trenches, but further down
the line they—well, this is what an R.A.M.C. man
told me. One day business took him thirty odd miles
into the back of the front, where he found himself in
a stronghold of one of the non-combatant corps of
the army—their name is legion. Talking to one of the
temporary inhabitants he was unwise enough to remark
that they seemed to have a nice safe spot to live in.
Immense indignation and a half-mile walk, until a
small hole in the ground was reached.

" See that ? "

" Yes."

" That's where we were bombed last June."

So perhaps we aren't the only people to run awful risks.

The frozen roads of yesterday are the quagmires of to-day, and where, last night, three lorries passed each other in comfort, one now tarries, mudded in up to the axles. In this war General Mud plays the part which used to be ascribed to General Janvier. You can't have any idea what it's like in the trenches, one moment everything fairly dry, the men cheerful, and the prospect of winning the war by 1920 quite in the picture. Then the rain starts, and from under their waterproof sheets the men look out at you as miserable as a collection of drowning rats, their feet splashing about in watery mud. At the back of every man's mind is the certain knowledge that he has no dug-out, that it is too wet to light a fire, and that the war will never end. As the rain trickles down their necks they wonder why they are paid a shilling a day for doing nothing. After all, they can't be a sixth part as valuable as the motor transport driver, back in his cosy billet trying to spend his six shillings a day. Not that life is roses, roses, all the way for them either, in fact there are very few people out here for pleasure, but it does strike the poor old foot soldier sometimes that it is funny that the further down the line you get the more you get paid for being there. And it's jolly hard to believe in the honour and glory of sitting still in a stinking ditch gathering unto yourself many years of rheumatism in the future.

We have started a divisional concert party now, the Woolly Bears they call themselves, after a particularly noxious type of Hun shell. There will be moments of heart-searching for some people thirty or forty years hence. Imagine, for instance, the feelings of X. when his grandson, from his perch on grandpa's knee, asks the fatal question, "And what did oo do in the gweat war, gwanpaw?" Will X. tell tales of derring do, or will he admit that he was the brunette of the —th Division Wind Ups? And will Y. in his dotage roll up his sleeve to show the scar, and tell tales of Loos? Or will he button it up and try and forget that he cut his arm while operating the cinema lantern? Will Z. glow with pride when he remembers how he used to wash the socks at the Divisional baths, and will Mrs. Q. ever know that her husband's, Captain Q.'s, experience of war was conducting nurses round the trenches at the training camp? I asks yer.

To-morrow we relieve the other brigade and begin to get on with the war again, so don't expect any letters for a long while from

Your

THOMAS.

The Shatoo,

December 6th.

Old Thing,

Have you ever lived in a Shatoo ? I guess not. Well, don't you be in a tearing hurry to do so. When I was very small I'm sure that someone taught me to believe that "le château" was French for "the castle." This place isn't the least bit like a castle, but it's a château all right. The map says so. Outside it is truly imposing, a fine white house, standing back from the road among trees and surrounded by an ornamental lake. Inside it is a cold and draughty barrack of a place, with horrible wall-paper and impossible sanitary arrangements. At the same time it is not everybody who can live in a château and call it "in the trenches," for this is our trench headquarters, and from it we sally forth every morning to perform "our daily round, our common task." We are well guarded too. We should be happier without the guns, though, for, where big guns are, there, sooner or later, are German shells. And so if some one came in the night and took Ermyntrude and Elisabeth, the 9.2's, away with him after throwing Deoch and Doris, the 6 inchers, into the lake, we would be prepared to grant him proficiency pay forthwith.

To reach the front gate you have to wade through a morass, and this is lucky for us, as we can see visitors long before they can get to us. Thus, when the

Divisional commander is spotted in the middle distance at 8.30 a.m. while we are still at breakfast, we have plenty of time to remove all signs of food from the table and make it look as if we had been at work for hours. Little he recks that the drawer marked Aeroplane Maps in reality contains the brigade major's scrambled eggs, or that the ordered disorder of the Staff captain's table hides a slice of toast. Of course it was a bit awkward when he sat down on the Brig's porridge nestling away under the *Times* on one of the chairs, but little things like that will occur in war time.

Later. Something awful has happened to my inside, and the doctor has been along and told me that I shall have to go to hospital, so I'm off to-night, and don't know when I shall be able to write.

Your
THOMAS.

CASUALTY CLEARING STATION,

December 7th.

Just a line to say that I have reached the Clearing Station and am going down the line by the next train, which shows the determination of the British race, for there is nothing the matter with me (my inside suddenly healed itself in the ambulance), but they have said that I must go down the line, and go I must, whether there is anything wrong or not. Not that I mind the holiday, but you feel a bit of a fraud when you find yourself packed away among the wounded.

They have given me a pair of pyjamas, the upstairs of which were intended for a young " gent " and not for a full-grown one. The downstairs of them, however, make up for any deficiencies in the upper stories, and Goliath would have felt lost in them.

I will keep this until I can let you know my permanent temporary address.—T.

December 9th.

I have landed on my feet all right this time, and am in a beautiful bed in the " Petits chevaux " room of the Paris Plage Casino. It was a bit of a disappointment at first to find out that none of the fairies who attend to my (imaginary) ailments were duchesses, but they are *bon* girls, and perhaps it would have been rather a bore to have to address your tooth-water bearer as " Your Grace," or whatever they call themselves.

One particularly charming one came up to me this morning and asked me something which I couldn't quite catch, but as she seemed to want to know if I was feeling bad I replied in the negative. It turned out that she was asking me whether I could wash myself, and as I had said " No," she insisted on washing me all over. Most embarrassing I call it.

Shall have to knock off now as tea is coming. We feed once in every two hours.

December 11th.

Am up and about now, and going up the line again to-morrow. The chief sight of this place is to be seen in the reading-room, where two convalescent lieutenant-colonels spend the whole day at a large jig-saw of Queen Victoria. If anyone speaks both the old fellows look up and glare at the offender as if to say, " Do you know that you are disturbing us ? " and if anyone approaches within several feet of their precious table they get warned off pretty quickly. At present, and for the last four days, one special piece has been exercising them greatly. Find it they cannot. " It's most extraordinary where that bit can have gone," says one, to which the other replies, " And it ought to be so easy to find a piece of that colour too." What would they say if they knew that the left eye of Queen Victoria was reposing in the pocket of the temporary second lieutenant who sleeps next to me ? He took it one day when they were at lunch.

It took an awful lot of talking to make the people here believe that there was nothing wrong with me, and I think that they have got the impression that I am really very ill in a hidden sort of way, but that I am repressing it in order to be sent up the line again to fight the Hun. Only people as far down the line as this could harbour an idea like that.

Good night.

Your

THOMAS.

A Railway Carriage,
Somewhere in France,

December 12th.

Darling,

Weep with me, for I am in the toils of the great
red tape machine and am gradually freezing to death
in this carriage as it crawls on its tired way to Rouen.
From Paris Plage I was pushed off to Étaples, where
I was left to languish for a whole day for no apparent
reason except that I was newly out of hospital and
very liable to catch pneumonia in the tent wherein I
lay. This morning I left for the Front in charge of a
draft, and laden with Movement Orders, Nominal
Rolls, and similar piles of waste paper. When I say
left for the Front, what I really mean is, set off in a
direction as nearly opposite to the right one as possible,
and am now on a short tour of France in a refrigerator.
Thus to get to Belgium I have to go down to Rouen,
and from there back through my starting-point to the
front. The only useful purpose I can be performing
is to air this terrible carriage, and surely that is a
work that women and children could do just as well.
As you may gather, I am not in a very good temper,
and so I suppose I had better leave off until such time
as a fire and a good meal have cheered me up.

Think I've recovered sufficiently from my fit of depression to carry on. I have now settled down for good at the Base Detail Camp, at least it doesn't seem as if they are ever going to let me away.

Here we rise and have breakfast in time to get on parade at nine. On the first day I strolled on gaily, little knowing what was awaiting me. There were about half a dozen of us officers and eleven hundred men, drafts to about twenty different battalions, drawn up in mass. After the usual preliminaries the adjutant of the camp turned round and asked which of us was senior. It seemed that I was. Would I then be good enough to march the battalion down to the central training ground. Think of it, and I hardly able to remember the right moment to say " Number 14 platoon, by the right, quick march." I had no more idea of what to do with a battalion than a mackerel would with a pair of water-wings, but it seemed to be a fairly safe thing to do to call them to attention. So, " Battalion—'Shun." No one seemed to pay any attention.

" It's not a secret," remarked the adjutant bitingly, " try and whisper it a bit more loudly."

This time I fairly shrieked it out, " BATALYUN— 'SHUN."

They 'shunned.

Made bold by my success, I tried another move, " SLOWUP—ARRMS."

About half of them did and the other half didn't,
they just stood there and grinned.

" Can't you see that half the men belong to rifle
regiments ? " from the adjutant.

" Er-m-yes."

This was very interesting, but hardly a time for
small chat about the men's units.

" Don't you know that they don't slope arms ? "

" Can't they ? "

" No rifle regiment does."

" Oh," said I, " then tell me how I ought to talk to
them."

He did, and we moved off, me at the head.

The training ground is a large sandy plain, skirted
on two sides by a pine forest which stretches away for
miles and miles. Here, while the men go through a
rigorous course of training, officers can attend a
lecture on trench warfare, throw live bombs, or be
instructed in the machine gun. I have heard, and
seen, all that I ever want to of trenches, and I'm not
keen on throwing bombs under the guidance of a
man whose only claim to be teaching the subject is
that he isn't well enough to be up the line. Therefore I have been a regular attendant at the machine
gun lectures and know already that the lever on the
Maxim gun pulls forward, while that on the Vickers
pulls back, or vice versa, I never can remember quite
which.

The town isn't half such a bad spot, and much amusement and good food can be obtained therein. Last

night we went to see a revue, but it was disappointingly proper.

Have to censor about seven hundred letters now. How these men do write when they come out first.

Cheero.

THOMAS.

THE "SHATOO"

THE "SHATOO".

CHAPTER VI

THE " SHATOO "

THE CHATEAU,

December 23rd.

DARLING,

Back to the front, and rather glad to be there, too, strange though it may seem. Just in time for Christmas in the trenches, and fatigue parties are out trying to find holly and other seasonable greens for the walls of the château. It hasn't changed much, the old shatoo, since my late departure, only a bit more dingy outside and a bit more musty in.

Did I ever tell you that I am Mess President? Though I says it as shouldn't, anyone less fitted for the job could hardly be imagined, with the exception of my predecessor, the late French interpreter. He had spent many years in Patagonia or Pamphylia or one of those outlandish spots, and had lived there entirely on sardines and raw mutton, until he had grown to have a devouring passion for them and for nothing else in the world. However, his King and country, or the French equivalent, needed him, and he departed for the less healthy atmosphere of a trench mortar battery, where his days are numbered, poor fellow.

The result is that if I dare to present either of these delicacies to my patrons there is a row. At present my chief trouble is the Christmas dinner. The plum pudding is all right, except that it will be hard to choose from the selection of them which is pouring in every day. The general has two, the brigade major three, the Staff captain one, and the rest of us five between us. How I am going to make them all imagine that they are eating one of their own I don't know, unless I take a desperate plunge and use the seven-pound one sent by the *Daily News*. It should be a pleasing sight, half a dozen stalwart Tariff Reformers eating the gift of that paper. After the pudding we have plenty of preserved fruits, as well as almonds and raisins, but the turkey looks like falling through, and heaven alone knows what will take its place. There is a large haggis, but of course that is being kept for Hogmanay night. I'd love to give them mutton, with sardines as the savoury, but I don't think I have the courage. We shall do all right in the liquid department, as we have been sent a dozen of champagne, and have some fine old port (à la Field Force Canteen) and a selection of liqueurs in our cellar. Our cellar, by the way, is a large packing-case which travels about with us wherever we go. Each time we move, a bottle of port or whisky gets smashed—" must have been the bumping on the road "—but it wouldn't look quite so suspicious if one of the bottles of mineral water got done in as well. Isn't it a terrible war ?

We have two orderlies to do the waiting and that

sort of thing. It sounds rather extravagant, but it isn't really, as one of them is too old to do anything else, and if we didn't have him he would have to go home as unfit. The head orderly stutters, but never smiles, and is constantly fighting with his helpmate, the infirm one, who goes by the name of Gibb. Gibb is a canny Scot, tall and skinny, with a flowing white moustache. He is very old, and claims to have fought in the Crimea, or one of those little shows of the early nineteenth century. He loves any sort of work which is unnecessary, and, though he is always at it, he won't do anything unless he does it in his own way. His chief jobs are to pick the tea-leaves out of the sugar (somebody down the line always mixes them up before we get them), and to remove the hairs from the crust of the bread. Ration bread is always covered in hair, for some reason or another. It rather looks as if the bakers rub the loaves in sandbags while they are still warm. He does those two jobs quite well, but where he is a bit of a trial is waiting at mess. Of course he is much older than any of us, including the general, but that is hardly a good reason for his taking part in the conversation as he hands round the soup. " My opinion," remarks our guest, a mere major-general, " is that the Germans are not yet nearly done for, and that——" " Mon," breaks in old Gibb, " d'ye no' ken whit yon Bottomley says? " and the major-general, unaccustomed to being addressed as " Mon " by a private soldier, collapses in his chair unable to speak or eat.

The journey from Rouen was uneventful, and we arrived at the camp of the draft I had been bringing up at about midnight. One of the men to whom I was talking complained of the quietness of everything. He thought that there should be more noise and excitement generally. I told him that he would get all the excitement he wanted soon enough. And he did. Hardly could they have got to sleep before a most horrible shindy started, and soon every gun for miles around was going hard. I had just reached the shatoo and was relating my experiences of the past fortnight when we suddenly noticed a sweet smell, but not so sweet that we wanted to go on smelling it indefinitely, for it was gas. Then we understood what all the trouble was. Our front was all right and couldn't feel any of the effects of it, but where we were, a mile or two back, it was quite strong blowing down, as we afterwards learned, from the direction of Hooge. Altogether it was about the biggest fiasco possible for old Fritz, because all that happened was that his brave infantry waiting to walk into Ypres found themselves being rapidly interred in their own trenches by our artillery, and the few who did get up and try to advance soon wilted away into corpses, which, of course, was all for the best.

Well, old thing, keep the Yule log burning, and have a good Christmas. We mean to, though there's going to be no palling up with the Hun this year. Private Peace and General Good-Will got gassed up at Hooge on the 19th; they hadn't been given tube helmets,

you know, but Father Christmas, aided by the R.F.A.,
is going to do his bit along the German front line.

Happy Xmas.

THOMAS.

New Year's Day, 1916.

DARLING,

Such excitement, a German aeroplane brought
down in the same field as our huts. We were sitting
down to breakfast, when overhead we heard the faint
pop-pop-pop of a machine gun and out we rushed.
Seven or eight thousand feet up, shining like silver
in the morning sun, was a Taube, making all out for
home with a great trail of steam shooting from its
exhaust, and behind it, but rapidly drawing up, was
one of our fighting planes. As we looked, our machine,
gathering up a terrific speed, passed over the German,
then turned round like lightning and was over it again,
and then circled round it, firing all the time. Suddenly
the Taube burst into flames and crumpled up. Down,
down it fell, faster and faster, and soon we could see
that it was coming very near us. With a swssssssssh it
came, as we all lay flat and hoped for the best, but it
landed a little heap of charred wood and iron a good
fifty yards away. We rushed over to see if anything
could be done for the pilot, but he was wanting nothing
but a quiet burial. Back Poperinghe way we could
see the victor volplaning down to his breakfast.

We were relieved last night just about the time that

1916 reported relief complete, and poor old bruised 1915 hobbled off to its permanent rest billet. The first sign of the relief comes in the morning, when the signalling officer of the other brigade arrives, and starts to take over the lines, and to go over those which have been newly laid. His signallers arrive soon after lunch, and half an hour later ours leave for camp, the first of the brigade to go. During the afternoon the machine gun and bombing officers turn up, either on horseback or else on foot from the corner at which a friendly motor lorry has dropped them. Soon they are poring over maps in which lines in all colours radiate from points where machine guns lie hidden, and lists of grenades held in the trenches and at the main stores. Before long their relief is finished and two more weary soldiers hit out for home. With much splashing our mess cart struggles through the mud, loaded high with food and " the cellar." I am rather afraid, too, that when it turns the corner out of sight the packs of all the batmen will be added to the pile. The general, his work done, sits and reads the *Times* over again, while in the office the brigade major and Staff captain are clearing up their papers and talking. Darkness is falling when, with much creaking, the baggage of the other people arrives, and soon from the direction of the kitchen comes the smell of frying onions. The purr of a motor is heard in the distance, and then the k-lop, k-lop, k-lop of feet being dragged out of the mud. The door opens, letting in a blast of cold air and three muffled figures, the brains of our relief. The two generals retire to their room, where they discuss defence schemes and the programme of work. Our general is thinking to himself that he almost wishes that he hadn't to go, because he knows that the other people will thoroughly mess up the magnificent results of a week of real hard work. Their general, on the contrary, finds that his worst forebodings were only too true, and that during the week he has been away we have done absolutely nothing. That's the way in the army. Nobody ever does any work but oneself, and yet they do say that two million sandbags are used every week. In the office there is an atmosphere of " gum boots thigh left in trenches " and " position of suspected M.G. emplacements." While the Staff captain is handing over lists of stores, the correctness of which he certifies with his tongue in his cheek, the brigade major is explaining what has happened during the week, what work has been done, what strafing attempted, and, generally speaking, how the war has been progressing. Dinner comes on, and the mess president of the incomers apologises to the brigadier of the outgoers for the poorness of the dinner, which as a matter of fact he knows to be a particularly good one. Just as coffee is being served a message comes in to say that two of the battalions have successfully completed their relief, and gradually other pink slips arrive, telling that one lot of men have sat down to watch for another week and that ours are squelching down the long, long trail home. Ten strikes, and there are still the machine gun company and one of the battalions unrelieved.

Our brig. yawns. He has had a long day. Soon we are all yawning. We have nothing to do, and are very tired; they want to get to bed and sleep so that they can be up early next morning. We both have to stay until that last battalion has finished its relief, for the machine guns reported shortly before eleven, and it is almost twelve now. The brigade major goes to the telephone and rings up. " Haven't you finished yet—think the party for 32 must have got lost—try and hurry them up—yes, I know it's very dark— right—good night—what's that—oh, thank you, same to you," then hanging up the receiver and turning to the general, " They aren't quite finished yet, sir, but they wish you a Happy New Year." We settle down again in our chairs and carry on with the yawning. An orderly brings in a pink form. The brigade major wakes up with a start. " That's all now, sir," and goes off to wire to the division. We collect our coats and prepare to leave, when the brigadier remembers a story he must tell. It is a very long one, but all stories have an ending. The door opens, letting out a ray of light into the dark night. Then it closes, and we plough our way towards the car, where the driver sits half frozen. Sleet stings our face and ears, and we bury our chins still further in our coats. A mile or so in front of us men will be standing out in it all night. We are the lucky ones without a doubt. And from the cross roads the Belgian battery bursts out into a new year's greeting. Ha-ppy-New-Year.

Your T.

CAMP,

January 6th

All packed and ready to go to the trenches, but the Staff captain is away and I am doing this job for him, and am going up in the car, so I have a spare half-hour in which to write.

During this last rest we have been doing a good deal of experimenting with a new bomb thrower, which, on account of its queer appearance, has been christened the Heath Robinson machine. Four men, if they are strong, can just carry it, and the same number are required to work it. It stands on a broad base and consists of masses of very powerful springs and slender wooden arms which break on every possible occasion. In fact it combines the weight of a large howitzer with the effectiveness of a pea-shooter and the accuracy of a P.mb.rt.n B.ll.ng. The first time that we tried to use it was very nearly fatal to several of us. We placed the machine in position, in accordance with the book of words, pulled levers, compressed springs, and generally went through the motions until we were " perspiring freely." Then with great pride we placed the bomb in the cup and all of us stood aside except the man who was to light the bomb and depress the firing lever. The bomb lit with a splutter, and the operator depressed the lever. Up soared the bomb, up, and up, and up. Straight up in fact. This wasn't quite what we had intended, as when a thing goes straight up it comes straight down, and we were directly below it. We stood there, stuck in the mud, and watched that brutal little thing go up and up, and then down, down, down, until it fell with a flop into the ground at our feet. We held our breath and waited for the end—only another second—now—er—er— p'raps it's a dud. And a dud it was, thank the Lord, or I shouldn't be here to tell the tale. However, it gave us wind up, and we decided to practise with dummies until we were a bit more certain in our aim. After half an hour or so five yards in a hundred was our greatest error, and so once more we started on live bombs. The first one tore out of the machine at a terrific rate and buried itself several feet deep in the ground about ten yards in front of us. Luckily it was imbedded so deep in Belgium that the ensuing explosion did us no harm, but there wasn't any great keenness to go on after that, though we had to carry on and give the thing a proper trial. The next shot went off almost at right angles and entered the camp of a grandfathers' battalion, where it slightly wounded one young chap of sixty-two. He was hugely braced, as he said that three of his sons and four of his grandchildren had already been in the roll of honour, and he was beginning to feel rather out of it. We stopped for the day.

The grandfathers' battalions are, I believe, technically known as labour battalions, and are recruited from men of over forty-two. To see the old dears marching along in what they call fours, dressed in their leather jerkins, with a spade over one shoulder and smoking clay pipes, is one of the most cheering sights of the war. They don't look like soldiers, and don't always address their officers as " Sir," but they stroll along to their work laughing and talking as pleased as Punch to be " doing their bit out here." And they do their work well too, road-making generally or digging reserve lines of trenches. They don't carry rifles or any unnecessary equipment, for which I should think they were only too thankful, although I did hear one old boy grousing because they sent them up somewhere they were likely to be shelled without rifles ! Most people would rather have had a spade I should think.

A frantic message came from the division the other day that several hundred old bombs which had been returned to the D.A.C. had been sent with their detonators still in, and as there are about two hundred and thirty-five regulations against this " practice," a Court of Enquiry was to be held to decide who was to blame. On the face of it things looked rather black for me, and so it was with a certain amount of trepidation that I attended the court and heard the evidence becoming more and more incriminating. The decision of the court was that somebody was to blame and that that somebody was me. As a last resort I suggested that we should go and see the bombs, for I was almost certain that I was guiltless. We went to an old barn where we found a guard placed to ward off any inquisitive persons from the danger zone, and amid shivers of excitement we went in and saw before us on the floor a heap of old rusted bombs, the mud of the trenches still thick upon them. "There you see," said the president, "detonators and all," and he pointed to something which protruded from the end of each bomb. This was awful, but in desperation I picked one up and looked at it. Then the laugh was with me, for what had put horror into the division was not a collection of detonators and fuses but some little bits of wood. The bombs were of a very old kind, in which little bits of wood take the place of detonators until they are ready to be fused, and what with the mud and the rust and the antiqueness of them the D.A.C. had got wind up quite needlessly. It was a relief to know that I shouldn't be shot at dawn after all.

The brigade major is rather proud of his horse, though as far as I can gather from equine experts it's nothing to write home about. On Wednesday there was a Divisional Horse Show, and he sent up his beast, though he couldn't go himself. In the evening it came back, and he announced to us that it had taken first prize. He went on to say that this proved his contention that it was no end of a charger, when the machine gun officer looked at the prize card. "What did you enter him as?" he asked. "An officer's charger," replied the B.M. indignantly. "Well, I only wanted to know because the card says First Prize for Light Draft Horses." Then we smiled, but not the B.M.

Cheero,

THOMAS.

THE CHATEAU,

January 14th.

PHYLLIS MINE,

I shouldn't start to pity me on account of " nights shivering in water-logged trenches." While you were writing that, what do you think I was doing ? List.

Night, and from a cloudless sky the moonbeams shed their silvery rays o'er the placid lake. Through the shadowy trees, shining white in the moonlight, stood the château. A door opened, and two figures could be seen, silhouetted against the warm glow of the room. The door shut, and footsteps crossed the frozen lawn to the lake. Arrived at the lake side the figures paused and looked around. " Just about here we left it, wasn't it ? " to which the answer, " Yes, here it is," and soon a dilapidated tub of a boat was being pushed into the water. " Got the spades, and the torches, and the revolvers?—right then, hop on while I hold the boat." Out into the silent pool sped the ship of mystery. Away round the corner it disappeared and nothing was left to tell of the grim armada save a few silver ripples on the calm surface of the water. All was still. Suddenly there was a shout, and stabs of white light began to play around the banks of the lake. There was an ominous crack, followed by a second, and then by still a third. The revolvers were getting to work. Then another cry and a splash, and save for the distant rattle of a

machine gun all was quiet. But not for long. Again
a shout and the flashing lights, and again the bark of
a revolver—crack, crack, crack, crack, crack. A few
minutes later the boat glided round the corner and
was beached. The two figures disappeared across the
lawn. The door opened and closed. All was still. Inside the interpreter pushed his chair a bit further from
the fire to make room for the two who had just entered.
" Well," said he, " and did you 'ave the *bonne chance?* "
" The how much? " " What you call the good fortune,
is it not? " " Oh, not so dusty. I got one with my revolver, and he got two, as well as one he hit on the head
with a spade. I wish we had some proper oars though,
because spades are rather difficult things to row with
at night." The speaker went to the door and opened
it. The stillness of the night was broken by a p-lop as
a water-rat dived into the lake. " Don't seem to have
killed them all," said the Staff captain, looking up
from his desk.

So you see we are not without our little pleasures.

But next morning the Brig. wanted to know who
had put a revolver bullet through his bedroom window.

To-day I have spent down in the middle sector of
our trenches, a place which used to figure too frequently
in our *communiqués* early in the spring. The trenches
there are Cambridge blue with a little grey in it, and
so are you after a journey through them. It will hardly
be giving away any great secret to tell you that this
is caused by the mining which has been going on for
more than a year, in fact on one five hundred yard

square of the map there are no less than thirteen mine
craters marked, and if you look over the parapet you
can see them, or some of them. It is said that two
worthy Scotchmen who celebrated Hogmanay night
rather too well made a complete tour of them in the
early hours of New Year's Day, singing Auld Lang Syne.
What else happened in those " Witches' Cauldrons,"
to quote from the German, is wropt in mystery, but
the two came back just as it was becoming light with
two old chairs and a young Hun who had done still
better than they in the festivity line.

I must away. "Hoppin' this finds you as it leevs
me in the pink,"

Your
THOMAS.

IN CAMP,

January 20th.

MY HAT, PHYLLIS,
    Talk about sleuth hounds. Yesterday we were
warned that a tall dark spy was thought to be going
round the trenches dressed in the uniform of an R.E.
officer. We wired round to all the battalions to keep
a good look out for the suspect, and then we forgot all
about it and went on with the day's work. Just as
we were sitting down to tea there was a knock at the
door which leads into the garden, and in marched four
brawny Scots with a prisoner, the tall dark man
dressed in the uniform of an R.E. officer. Before any

of us could speak the office door opened and admitted a guard of Yorkshiremen with a captive. " Ah've copped him," cried the leader. The captive was the tall dark man dressed in the uniform of an R.E. officer. From the direction of the kitchen came sounds of scuffling, and the door burst open. There stood two Welshmen; armed to the teeth. In between them was the tall dark man dressed in the uniform of an R.E. officer. Instinctively we turned to the one remaining door, and sure enough it gave way, and through it came three excited Londoners and their prize. We all knew how it would be. Their prize was the tall dark man dressed in the uniform of an R.E. officer. A signaller came in. " Message from the division, sir." The message read, " With reference to spy, it is now reported that he is short and fair, and not tall and dark as previously reported." Our four prisoners had tea with us. They all belonged to the same Field Company.

The spy was eventually caught by the Canadians, who are quite close to us, so close in fact that we share a communication trench with them. Some time ago I was taking a Cook's tourist round the trenches. Cook's tourists, by the way, are the people who are sent out for a few days to see war, chiefly people in home service brigades. This particular one was a major, and he had very foolishly neglected to bring anything but thin boots with him. As I have already said, I was detailed to take him round, and in due course we arrived at this communication trench. Half-way down it became very wet, about eight inches of water with a good bit of mud underneath. Standing on the one dry spot was a Canadian in beautiful long thigh gum boots in which he could have waded knee-deep without getting wet. As we drew near I began to wonder what he would do. If he continued to stand there my major would have to paddle through the slime. If he got off into the mud himself we should pass dry. What do you think happened?

There is a proposal to give all officers and men who have been wounded some distinguishing sign, as they do in the French Army. We have to solicit proposals from the battalions, and some of them wax very humorous indeed about it. One suggestion is that a large purple patch should be worn on the spot where the wound occurred, but it would look bad, wouldn't it? to see a man going along with a patch of purple, say, on the seat of his breeches. It would cast grave doubts as to the part which the hero was taking at the time he was wounded, pursuer or pursued. There are all sorts of other suggestions, but the whole thing seems to be rather unnecessary. It isn't as if there were any special merit in getting wounded, and many people who have never been hit deserve badges far more than some who have. Take, for instance, the man who has been out since the beginning but has had the fortune, or should I say misfortune, never to be hit. Hasn't he earned a badge more than the man who is slightly wounded the first day he ever goes near the trenches ? And the man who is seriously wounded, surely he ought to have a bigger badge than the man who is only slightly hit. And so on, and so on, though why they should want to give us badges at all heaven alone knows. Still I see that "the paper that foretold the war" says we want them, so I suppose we must.

Getting up this morning I heard two men arguing outside. Said the first, ". . . so I throws it into the destructionerator, and . . ." "You don't know what you're talking about," broke in the other, "what you mean is the inspectorator . . ." and they kept at it until my servant came in with my boots, so I asked him what all the trouble was about. Nothing at all it seemed, except that they were both trying to say "insinuator." "Insinuator," I asked in amazement, "what's that?" "Don't you know, sir?—the thing they burn the rubbish in."

Good night.

Your

Thomas.

In Camp,

January 25th.

Dear Old Thing,

Thanks so much for the magazines. I loved the story in which the grocer's assistant, temporary private, penetrated the German lines all by himself and captured a heavy battery single-handed. The whole thing was so realistic. Take, for example, the behaviour of the platoon commander when he hears a shell coming. As far as I can remember he acts somewhat as follows : " Platoon, 'shun ! Now, my men, you can no doubt hear approaching through the air some heavy body. It is a shell of seventy-two calibres " (whatever that means), " and if it continues to travel uniformly at its present velocity it will impinge upon the surface of the ground in seventeen and a half twentieths of a second. Slope arms ! Let us show the enemy that we are not afraid of the worst he can do to us. Present arms ! " Or words to that effect, but probably you read it yourself. Well, if I know any-thing about it, what that officer said was just plain, " Oh, hell ! " as he flopped unceremoniously on the ground and waited for the bump.

We went to see the concert party in Pop last night. It has been going now for well over a year and is top-ping. At one time they used to " feature " (good word that) two real French girls, but I imagine that they became too independent, and now the fair young thing in a short skirt and filmy *crêpe de Chine* un— deletions by the censor, I mean, is a corporal in the A.S.C. Their forte is parody, and I wonder what the composer of " The Temple Bells " would think if he heard the woeful tale of the man who

> Stole our tot of rum,
> Rrum, rrrum, rrrrum,
> Rrum, rrrum, rrrrum.

Did you ever hear that song, " There's something

in the seaside air "? Well, these people have discovered that " There's something in the Belgian beer," though what it is (bar mud) I've never been able to find out. There was another touching little ditty about a certain " Bo-Peep," who " resided in Ypres, resided in Ypres," but eventually she found out, like many of us have in this war, that there's more doing in Rouen than in little Belgium, and so she flitted, and is now where she can doubtless find many willing little lambs. But the tit-bit of the show came at the end, when the B.E.F. version of the Bric-a-Brac song, " The Optimist and the Pessimist," was sung by two pseudo gendarmes, one fat and jolly and the other wilted and woeful. They were dressed in the most priceless uniforms, probably purloined from some deserted *gendarmerie*, and were a cross between the gala rig-out of a full-blown admiral and the gilded splendour of the man who stands outside the cinema. Throughout the optimist had all the best of it, and the pessimist was never out of trouble. When a new M.O. came on the scene it was the optimist who managed to wangle indefinite " excused duty," while the poor pessimist, really ill, was enjoined not to " swing the lead," and was given M. and D. (medicine and duty), and of course the inevitable number nine. But perhaps it was his own fault for suggesting that the M.O. did not " know his jo-er-ob." In the next verse the optimist has again fallen on his feet and is spending his time in the well-stocked canteen, while the poor pessimist has been detailed for a digging fatigue of a particularly undesirable nature. And so it goes on through several encores, until at last they find one point on which they do agree. Both think that " the man who says that he likes bombs must be a bl-blooming fool," and the song ends on a cheerful note, even from the pessimist, whose relief when the culminating shell proves to be a dud is truly pathetic to behold. A ripping evening. You leave the hall and go out into the night. In front of you is a signboard dimly lit up by an oil lamp. " To Ypres," you read.

The following story is going round. I won't vouch for the truth of it. Nine heroes upon whom France has bestowed the Legion of Honour were sent down to the base to receive the decoration at the hands of a French general. They were rather surprised to be met at the station by an ambulance, but the driver assured them that it was all right. Their surprise at this, however, was nothing to what it became when they stopped at a hospital and were told to go inside. Here they waited for a short time until a man in a flowing white coat told them to follow him. They followed meekly, and before they knew quite what was happening they were being inoculated for typhoid. At about the same hour a thrilling scene was being enacted in the principal square of the town. Nine officers, standing bolt upright at attention, were being embraced by a passionate general. On the breast of each of them shone the coveted Croix. And none of them could understand what on earth it had all got to do with the inoculation for which they had come. What about

" The path of duty " being " the road to glory " now ?

That's all for to-day, thank you.

Your

THOMAS.

THE CHATEAU,

February 1st.

FAIR ONE,

We've had a visit from the Navy since I wrote last. They came for two days and then left us, without regrets as far as life in the trenches was concerned. One afternoon we heard that several petty officers and men were on their way from divisional head-quarters, and that they were to be sent up into the trenches. We wired to the battalions to prepare to receive boarders, and then sat down and waited for our guests.

Tea-time came and no sailors. Dinner, and nothing had been heard of them. Coffee, and they arrived, mud from head to foot, and very tired. A mile out from divisional headquarters their bus had grown contrary and tipped them out into several feet of Belgian mud at the roadside. It had then lain down and refused to be pulled out, and so the poor chaps had to disembark and proceed on foot. They evidently weren't accustomed to the roads we patronise in this part of the world, and the slippery *pavé* and the mud had been too much for them. They were dressed in khaki with the blue band of their ship round the cap, but they had thought the peaks of the caps unsailorlike and had cut them off. When they had swallowed a certain amount of the liquid refreshment they became quite communicative and wanted to tell us again and again all that had befallen them, but we had to send them off soon, as their journey up to the trenches was still in front of them. They didn't seem at all keen to leave the warmth of brigade H.Q. for the more doubtful pleasures of a trench, and they arrived up at the battalions dead to the world. And no wonder. They had two days of weather quite up to sample, and left us wet through and longing to get back to their ships.

Did you see in the paper a few days ago about the Hun blowing us up by the Canal ? I went there last night just to have a look, although it isn't in our brigade sector, but I thought it would be interesting to see, and besides the old battalion was holding the trenches there. So I started off after dinner and had a topping time. You would hardly know the place—of course you wouldn't—I mean I could hardly recognise it, so much had it changed since we were there in August. The trees which I knew as trees are now mere stumps, and the stumps I knew as stumps are now little splinters lying here and there all over the place. Right at the point of the mound there is an enormous crater, far bigger than the Hooge one, and to look down from the top of the mound to the bottom of the crater at its foot is almost a hundred feet. To get to the trenches round the crater you have to go through a long, long tunnel about four feet square right through the centre of the mound, and then you come out not far from the top, so you have to descend by one of the quaintest bits of trench I have ever seen. It drops almost perpendicularly into the trench below down the side of the mound, and as it is in full view of the enemy it has been covered over with brushwood and broken logs and pieces of rotted sandbag, so that it is absolutely hidden. In dry weather you can slide down it into the trench, and in wet weather you can't help doing so. It was wet when I went. Another little trouble is that it is only two foot deep at present, and unless you bend almost double your head breaks through the pseudo-foliage and a German bullet breaks through your head. On my way back I fell into a shell hole head over heels, and came out rather chilly. I distinctly heard the ice crack as I plumped in. Oh, it was horrible walking home with my clothes gradually freezing on me, but I found that by running I could work up enough warmth to keep the ice from actually forming. It was about 3 a.m. when I crawled into bed, such as it is, and it is now eight, and I am waiting for my servant to bring me up some breakfast. Then I hope to be able to get another hour or two's sleep before getting up. So cheero till this afternoon.

The Evening.

It was nearly cheero for ever. After breakfast I went to sleep again, according to plan. Some hours later, I can't exactly say when, but it must have been about eleven, I was woken up by a large lump of shell crashing through the window, and coming to rest with a bang against the wall. I jumped out of bed like lightning and looked out. There in the middle of the garden were six bright new shell holes, and strung out across the field in front was brigade headquarters making at full speed for a dug-out in a field far away from all shells, and where we had an alternative telephone station through which we could keep in communication with our front. I dashed on a coat and a pair of gum boots and joined them scantily dressed. From them I heard that the Hun had been bombarding the surroundings of the château for an hour, while I must have been fast asleep. Of course they were not trying to hit us. It was the guns all round us that they were after, but German shells, especially when propelled from their guns by Landsturmers, don't always hit what they are aimed at. We sat there till three o'clock watching our beloved château and expecting to see the last of it every minute, but it escaped marvellously, and except for a few scratches took no more harm from it than we did. Oh, but it was cold.

Good night.

T.

THE CHATEAU,

February 5th.

PHYLLIS MINE,

If you have thrills to thrill, prepare to thrill them now. The morning broke fine but foggy, and I went forth to war. When I reached the front line the fog had grown still more pea-soupy, with the result that it was possible to go right out in front of the parapet and have a good look at the wire and the night listening posts without danger of being spotted. So out I climbed, for there was one post, on the edge of a small crater, which I was anxious to see by daylight. As the journey was rather an arduous one, and not expecting to meet any of the enemy, I left my revolver and everything behind and strolled out. Every little detail for ten yards or so around was quite clear, but further than that all was lost in the mist. I made for the post and jumped in. After I had made a thorough inspection and seen that the bombs and things were all right, I climbed out on to the top, and was just going to make off for home when to my amazement and dismay I saw two Huns not ten yards away, standing on the opposite lip of the crater. What was I to do, alone and unarmed? They had not seen me, but were apparently intent on a search for souvenirs while they had the chance. I decided to creep away and return with my revolver and a couple of men, but before I had time to move the nearer of the two turned round and saw me. For a second he stood there, looking as if he had seen a ghost. He was tall and fair, and on his head was the usual little red and grey pill-box cap. But what scared me most was that in his hand was a rifle. His comrade, noticing that something was up, looked round too, and I could make out the features of his nasty, dirty little face with its three days' beard. The whole thing can't have taken more than a second, but it was a ghastly one for me. To provide target practice for two Huns at ten yards' range is a poor death. But I was not meant to die. Urged by a common impulse those two Huns dropped their rifles and beat it. Talk about a lucky providence, but I'm going to take a revolver next time. You can imagine, too, that I also ran once I found myself alone, for I knew that those valiant Teutons would raise the alarm directly they got home, and hardly had I clambered back into the front line when a burst of rapid fire broke out along their line. I wonder how those two explained the loss of their rifles.

A certain officer in a certain battalion in this brigade has for a long time been on the look out for a soft job, and it was with great joy that he heard the other day that he had been appointed divisional massage officer. Before ten minutes he had distributed the good news among his friends that he had been given an appointment on the divisional Staff. The fact that he was ignorant of the first principles of massage did not trouble him in the least. It was a cushy job. The morning he spent in writing to a celebrated tailor for three tunics of superior workmanship, and a pair of the very pinkest of pinky-yellow riding breeches. A bootmaker in town had an order for a pair of the latest thing in field boots. In fact our hero was determined to be worthy of the division which had recognised his merit. In the afternoon he reported, according to order, at divisional headquarters. He was shown into the D.A.A. and Q.M.G., who did not welcome him with outstretched arms, as of course he should, but went on writing for ten minutes. Then he looked up. " What do you want ? " he asked. The latest member of the Staff disclosed his identity, whereupon the D.A.A. and Q.M.G. explained what his duties would be. " You know V——" He did, and his face fell. It was a village a few hundred yards in rear of the firing line much loathed by the Hun. In fact they loathed it at least three times a day with 5.9's. That was why his face fell. " Well, you'll live there in a cellar with four R.A.M.C. men, and you will issue dry gum boots to the men going up into the trenches and collect the wet ones from the men as they come out. All men who look as if they are going to suffer from trench foot will be sent to you to have their feet rubbed and soaked in oil. I am afraid it isn't a particularly nice job, but some one has got to do it, and I believe you expressed your willingness to take on any job. Oh, by the way, the R.A.M.C. men will be relieved once a week, but you will have to stay on permanently. Sorry, but it can't be helped. Good-bye." The moral of which is, I suppose, " Let well alone." I wonder what the poor chap will say, though, when his pink breeches and his last word in field boots reach him in the Divisional Massage Station, a damp and dangerous cellar, infested by rats and crumps.

There is some word of our going back for another rest, but it seems early days yet.

Cheero.

THOMAS.

IN REST,

February 15th.

DEAR GIRL,

As was rumoured, a rest was in store for us. We were pulled out of the line without much warning, and here we are in a dear old village resting for all we are worth. We arrived at a station eight or nine miles away, and marched here through the snow, first of all along the level, then through a great black wood as still as death, and then down into this village, nestling round the church, with the walls of the cottages almost as white as the snow itself, and the most gorgeous red tile roofs. Everything seemed so peaceful as we halted in the square and waited to be shown our billets. A perfect rest. Breathless rides through those grand woods. Pleasant afternoons round the fire. Of such things we thought. And there were rumours of a trout stream and a beautiful gamekeeper's daughter —the beautiful daughter of a gamekeeper I mean. Our hopes have been dashed to the ground. We are resting in the manner prescribed by the powers that be, and not in our own way. The result is that we have never been busier in our lives.

This is what happens. After many months of red war a division is withdrawn to recuperate at some spot in rear of the line. Officers and men are tired. They need a rest. Very well, they shall have one. And so they leave the guns behind them and seek repose. Now the land into which they come is a pleasant land, and a land where no Hun dwells. His place, however, is taken by the Arch-Hun, an old gentleman with a red band round his hat and nothing to do but to worry poor fatigued soldiermen. Before we have even had one good night's sleep Arch-Hun Number One descends upon us. He earnestly hopes that we shall have a good rest, but we must realise that we are where we are not only for the purpose of resting, but also in order to smarten ourselves up again, and recover from the discipline devastating effects of trench warfare. We salute and promise to do an hour's close order drill every day. As he leaves the room, Arch-Hun Number One collides with Arch-Hun Number Two, who is on his way to impress upon us the need of long route marches for troops who have been unable to move about for the past few months. We give him our word for it that we had intended to have a route march every day, and we pray fervently that the other Arch-Huns have an offensive or something to keep them busy and leave us in peace. But we pray in vain. Number Three we never saw, but he spoke to us over the phone. He said that he was in command of the training area or something of that sort, and was no end of a general. We did not stand to attention as he couldn't see us, but when he rang off we were committed to an hour's running and rapid marching before breakfast. Arch-Hun Number Four was convinced that Physical Jerks were essential to the welfare of troops in rest, and Number Five thought that we must have forgotten how to skirmish and wouldn't it be a good thing if we did some every day just to freshen up the memories of the men. Arch-Hun Number Six was of the old familiar kind, from whom we cannot escape even when we are not resting. He desired the presence of fifty men every day at the Coal dump at B24c85 from eleven to two to unload coal. Arch-Hun Number Seven thought that another little inspection wouldn't do us any harm, and Arch-Hun Number Eight, who should really be classed as Super-Hun Number One, put the lid on it by stating that, as the training which must be put in by us during our rest period was so important for all ranks, leave would be stopped, but that as a special favour one per cent of the strength might be allowed to go on a jaunt to Calais for twenty-four hours. Aren't they good to us ?

So here we are resting hard from about 3.30 a.m. till late in the day. One witty adjutant suggested that in order to save the breath of his pet bugler Lights Out and Réveillé should be blown at the same time, as otherwise they couldn't be expected to get through all the work.

On the whole we prefer the common or garden Hun to the Arch ditto. There are wire entanglements in between him and us.

Cheero, I must run away and rest—at the bombing trenches—for a few more hours.

Your

THOMAS.

ALARUMS AND EXCURSIONS

CHAPTER VII

ALARUMS AND EXCURSIONS

STILL IN REST,

February 26th.

DARLING,

I'm so sorry I haven't been able to write before, but the Staff captain has been away on leave and I have been doing his job as well as my own, and as the last few days have been times of rumours and false alarms, sudden calls and still more sudden wash-outs, I haven't had a minute to spare.

The battalion has gone. After exactly a year in this good old division it has left to rejoin the crowd to which we really belong and which came out some three months after us.

The white expanse of snow was relieved only by the unending avenue of black trees which stretched as far as the eye could see, the road which leads away from Flanders. From the angry grey sky the snow fell in great eddying gusts, clinging to the coats of the men who stood there and settling on the flat tops of their packs. In the centre of the motionless khaki square stood the man who had given us our orders

179

during that great year. He had seen us come, raw but eager, and now he was here to say good-bye to us. He had finished speaking. The cheering was over. Down the hill, through the driving snow went the long column. At the head marched the band, the pipers playing that soul-stirring march " The Athol Highlanders," the drums crashing in with their weird accompaniment. Then came the specialists, machine gunners, snipers and bombers, the pick of the battalion, and then the four companies. Last came the transport, limber after limber, as clean and bright as a year ago, each dragged by a pair of strong mules, their hot breath clearly visible in the cold air. First the machine gun limbers, their death-dealing contents well covered with tarpaulins ; then the field kitchens, a trail of smoke escaping from their chimneys, and leaving behind a pleasant smell of " stew." Then the tool carts, and the supply wagons. A solitary rider, muffled up to the chin, and they were gone.

The battalion had gone. But it remains. From that closed gate to Calais, the Menin Road, by the devilish heights of Hooge ; through the shell-torn awfulness of Sanctuary Wood (grim jest) ; in Zillebeke ; and at Hill 60 ; upon the tree-shattered slopes of the Bluff ; and by the side of the once so peaceful canal they " stand fast," the invisible guardians of the desolate white towers of Ypres. Will the next page in their history equal the first ?

Phew, aren't I becoming journalistic ?

During the time we have been in rest we have had

all sorts of sports, steeplechases, soccer competitions, and last, but by no means least, boxing tournaments. The finals had a most dramatic climax. Imagine to yourself a great barn filled with benches, and in the middle a raised platform lighted by electricity obtained from heaven alone knows where. The barn is crowded to overflowing with officers and men, who come in rubbing their blue hands and shaking the snow off their coats. Outside it is freezing hard, and several inches of snow are on the ground. A corporal in the A.S.C. is down to box a bombardier in the R.F.A. in the last of the finals, the Heavyweights. The infantry have carried off most of the honours, but in this class the other branches of the Service have had it all their own way. The first round starts in silence, broken only by the padding of the boxers' feet, and the dull thud of a blow as it finds its billet. " Time," and they are lying on chairs while enthusiastic seconds flourish towels over them. " Time," and they are up again, but not for long. There is an instantly suppressed shout of excitement as one of the fighters collapses on the floor, knocked out by a shrewd blow just under the heart. " One-two-three-four-five-six-seven-eight-nine-ten. Bombardier More wins," and the finals are over. In the cheering and excitement which followed few noticed that a message was being passed up to the front. Suddenly a Staff officer jumps up on to the platform from which the victor is helping down the vanquished. He holds up his hand for silence. " The division has to move almost at once. Get back to

your billets every one as quick as you can and pack up."
Out in the clear moonlight night streams of men are
making their way across the snow. A dazzling light
shines in their eyes, as with a " honk, honk," a dispatch rider streaks past on his motor cycle. His head-
light plays weird tricks with the shadows of the trees.
Everywhere the same topic. If you have been holding
a sector of the trenches, and if while you are out for
a rest the Hun takes those trenches, and if you are
suddenly called up from your rest—well any fool can
put things like that together and get the right answer.
And when you have guessed the answer your heart
begins to thump a little bit louder, and perhaps there
are some who feel a tremor at the knees. But of course
that is due to the cold. War in the summer is hellish,
but in the winter it's worse. Hell at least possesses a
certain comforting warmth. And when everybody
had packed up, when I had issued several hundred
orders, mostly contradictory, and when the first battalion had actually started on its cheerless march to
the station through the snow, there came a message
cancelling the move. Which is a way we have in the
Army.

And now, after all these alarums and excursions, I
am pretty tired and am going off to my bed over the
butcher's shop.

Good night.

THOMAS.

A Belgian Pub,

March 3rd.

Darling,

We have moved at last, back near the old spot, and are now waiting for the order to go up and take over the recaptured trenches. The show seems to have been a great success, and one of the German prisoners is said to have remarked that as soon as they heard our division was on its way back they knew that the fur would start to fly. And it did " some," as the Canadians on our right would say.

Apparently the weather was so bad that the show had to be put off for a few days, and that was why our sudden move was still more suddenly cancelled. When we did move the weather had changed to a sort of early summer, and I had a most enjoyable journey in the hold of a motor lorry among the blankets, which, thank the Lord, had just come out of the Thresh disinfector, an antiquated sort of cross between a steam boiler and a trouser press into which clothes are placed for the purpose of denuding them of their parasitical population.

Our new billet is a pub, out of which we have turned a section of A.S.C., much to their annoyance, but with the express permission of a far higher authority. So that's all right, and they have departed in a flurry of field boots and bad language.

My farewell with the good man of my rest billet was truly pathetic. I went down to say farewell, and he

invited me to sit down and have a cup of coffee speci-
ally prepared for my benefit. This I did, and was just
about to take a sip when he checked me. "Un
moment, monsieur," and from a corner cupboard he
produced a bottle. "Cognac, monsieur," said he, and
then with a wink, "défendu. Monsieur comprit." I
compreed while he poured a liberal dose into my cup.
Then we began to converse. First we talked of Verdun,
at least he did, with the aid of a few "oui's" from me,
and then the conversation turned to the quality of his
meat, and from that again to his preference for Highlanders to any other species of "Tommee." Then
there was a pause until I brought my heavy guns to
bear. "C'est un terrible guerre," I remarked with my
most colloquial accent. That fairly set him off, and I
had no further need of talking before it was time for
me to go. I rose and bade him "Au revoir." He
replied that he hoped that I should never get "tiréd,"
to which I answered that "comme j'ai été au front
pendant plus d'un an j'espérais que, que, que . . ."
and broke down completely, but he seemed to understand what I was talking about, and we fell on each
other's necks in a fond embrace. Looking back upon
that parting, I think that the cognac must have been
very potent for me to let that old fellow place his arms
round my neck in the way he did. He was none too
clean.

We have all been served out with the new shrapnel
helmet, and now we look like so many Tweedledees.
(It was Tweedledee, wasn't it, who fought a battle

with a dish cover as helmet ?) Anyhow the tin hats are about the limit in ugliness, just like an inverted dish cover or tin basin, and when it comes to wearing them they are about as uncomfortable as they can be. They are all made in one size, presumably what the maker thought was the average size of Tommy's head, but he can't have had much admiration for their brains or he would have made them a trifle larger. Mine would only just balance in a sort of Charlie Chaplin way on my head until I took about half the lining out, and now I can wear it perched well on one side of my head in a manner which makes jealous generals stop and reprove me for trying to look too doggy, but, as I tell them, it can't be done any other way. Everybody looks so entirely different in them that sometimes you want to sit down and shriek with laughter, instead of which you have to stand bolt upright and salute, your inside rocking and all but splitting with pent-up merriment. They are jolly good things nevertheless, and if they had been started earlier would have saved thousands of lives.

Later. The order has come, and we are off to take over the trenches, so don't expect to hear from me for some time, as there will be lots to do. The fine weather of the last few days has come to a sudden end, and the snow is falling. You at home can have no idea of all that means to us.

Good-bye.

Your

THOMAS.

After a week which will always live in my memory
for the awful suffering which was going on around me,
we crawled home last night too despondent to do anything but fall down and sleep, curled up in our blankets,
without even removing our wet clothes. A few little
episodes from that time may give you a slight idea
of it.

We set out for the trenches in a borrowed car. The
weather was perfectly awful, and so we expected a
good many blocks on the road, but we never imagined
that we should arrive later than eight. We eventually
arrived at three next morning—walking. When we
started it was not four o'clock, but it was nearly dark.
Overhead masses of lowering grey snow clouds, on
either side fields deep in snow, and away in front of us
the road, a slippery ribbon of heart-breaking *pavé*, and
on either side of it mud, mud, mud, unfathomable mud.
Along this road, through the driving snow, crawled a
seemingly orderless herd of men and mules, lorries and
limbers. In the centre the *pavé* was crowded with
transport, all going in the same way, towards Ypres.
Nothing could have moved in the opposite direction,
for the *pavé* was barely wide enough for a single motor
lorry. Limbers full of rations, lorries coming up with
shells, wagons loaded up with timber, barbed wire,
and sandbags, followed each other with hardly a score

of inches between the tailboard of one and the steaming nostrils of the mules of the next. And in this funereal procession we had to take our place. Beside us plodded a platoon of infantry, their feet sinking deep into the mud at every step; wet, cold, and altogether miserable. It was bad enough for us in our car. It must have been awful for them. Suddenly, suddenly is a bad word, for we were only travelling at about two miles an hour, the limber in front of us stopped with a jerk. Momentary pauses were common, but after standing still for several minutes I got out of the car to see what had happened. A hundred yards up the road a lorry had side-slipped and was stuck with its front wheels fast in the mud at the side of the road and the rear several feet out into the middle of the *pavé*. This made it practically impossible to pass, but an ammunition limber bringing up urgently needed shells, and already very late, decided to chance it, and urging his horses to a canter, the driver dashed straight for it. A few yards from it they swerved, the near wheels sinking deep in the mud as they left the *pavé*, but their impetus carried them past, and with another swerve they were on to the *pavé* again, and trotting off in the distance. We get a bit restive sometimes when we see the Royal Regiment bringing up one officer's kit in a six-horse limber at a trot while we poor infantry have to be content with two mules to draw our heavily loaded wagons at a walk, but if it leads to driving like this you can forgive them. The next limber, loaded up with rations, tried to get past in the same way, but its

mules were either not strong enough or not well
enough driven, and, the rear half of the limber sticking
in the mud, the front half swung across the road, the
mules stumbled and fell into the ditch on the right,
and there was the whole road blocked. The lorry had
to be unloaded before it could be coaxed on to the road
again, and while this was done several pairs of mules
were untraced from limbers in the rear and were con-
nected up with the one which had fallen across the
road. With much swearing of drivers and creaking
of harness the fore part shifted, and then with a sudden
rush they tried to pull out the rear half from the mud.
For a few yards it ploughed its way along, the wheel
scraping against the side of the road, but refusing to
come up on to the *pavé*. Then with a crack the wheel
bròke. The only thing to do was to off-load the limber
and push it into the ditch, where, for all I know, it
still lies. The road was now clear and on we went.
Soon we caught up the weary infantry and passed
them, but when we reached a village where two con-
verging lines of traffic meet we were held up again.
And so on. When we did at last reach the cross roads
where the transport turns off for the trenches it was
nearly eleven o'clock, and the weather was worse than
it had been before. The road was of much the same
kind as the one from which we had turned, but narrower
and smashed to bits by shell fire. To add to the difficulties, on one side of the road there had once been a
light railway, and now the shattered rails threw up
their jagged edges out of the mud. Our car plunged

headlong into a shell hole and refused to move. Neither backward nor forward could it stir. Some men stumbled towards us from the trenches, falling into holes every few paces and picking themselves out again without complaint, too tired even to swear. Wet through from head to foot, footsore and utterly weary, these were a few of the men who, the day before, had taken part in the most gallant and probably the most successful enterprise of the year, heroes if you like. But not much glory about it for them as they stagger home. Though they were so absolutely done, they offered to help us, and help us they did, but to no purpose. So we left the car and started to walk along the road, or rather along the field by the side of it. The road itself was the most wonderful and at the same time one of the most awful sights I have ever seen. Though smaller than the first road we had been on, and though crumpled up by shell fire, it was necessary for two lines of traffic to be on it at the same time. For one limber to move along that road by itself by daylight would have required good driving. For two unending streams to do so in the middle of a dark winter's night with a blizzard blowing was obviously impossible. But it was being done, because it had to be done. And, mind you, one of the two streams had to plough its way through the mud. It was magnificent to see the way in which those drivers dashed through mud over the axles of their heavily loaded limbers. And the way in which their mules responded was magnificent too. Sometimes the foreleg of one of them would crash against a piece of the broken railway line, and with a whinny of dismay the poor animal would collapse in the mud. There would be a shout for the transport officer. In a few moments you would see a dim figure leaning over the struggling mule, and then there would follow the crack of a revolver. Soon the stream would be dashing through the morass again, but this time over the body of a mule. The men in the trenches got their rations. The bombs arrived to fill up the depleted stores. By the light of guttering candles the holders of the front line read the letters from their wives and sweethearts, crouching together in their low and damp dug-outs. And if there were a few dead mules along that ghastly road there were many dead men up on that dread snow-swept, shell-torn Bluff.

Three days after the relief a sentry thought he heard a voice out in front of the parapet. At night a patrol went out. Into the mud up to his armpits they found a creature, starving, frost-bitten and speechless. He was taken to the dressing station, where his clothes were taken off and he was wrapped in a blanket and placed before the fire. The man who undressed him noticed some peculiarity about his tunic, and scraped the mud off a portion of it. He found that it was grey and not khaki. The man in front of the fire was a German. When he had been given something hot to drink the M.O., who happened to be a fluent speaker of German, questioned him. This was his story. On the day of the attack he with two comrades had hidden in a shell hole with the intention of escaping back to the German lines at night, but when night came, so vigilant were the sentries on both sides, they dared not, and so they stayed there for another day until, driven by hunger, they had started. The other two had been slightly ahead of him. As they went the mud became worse and worse, snow and thaw for four days, and after a time they could make no progress. They tried to turn round and get back to the shell hole, but that also they found impossible. He managed to catch hold of a tree-stump, but his two companions, less fortunate, felt themselves sinking. They struggled, but their struggles only caused them to sink still further, until at last the mud closed in round them and all that was left was one hand, blue with cold, pointing to the sky. Can you imagine a more awful death? The gratitude of the prisoner was, I believe, quite pathetic, and when he left the dressing station he tried to tip the M.O. two pfennigs, the total wealth that he possessed.

This was only one instance of men getting lost in the mud, and on several occasions it took as many as twenty men pulling at an armoured telephone cable to pull one poor devil out, and when at last the mud yielded him up it would be without his boots, and several times I saw men who had been pulled out like this crawling down to the dressing station with bare feet through the mud and snow. Oh, it was horrible.

I was on my way to a certain trench. It was mud over the knees, and I could hardly make any headway.

I met a Tommy carrying down a badly wounded man. We passed. Five minutes later—about fifty yards separated us then—there was a terrific explosion, and a shell burst behind me. I ducked. When it was over I looked round. The Tommy was still carrying his burden, but from his own thigh there poured a stream of blood. He had been hit by the shell. He knew as well as I did that his best chance of life was to leave the wounded man and get to the dressing station as fast as he could. But he stayed, and agonising step by agonising step he carried his pal towards help. How will that man be remembered ? As a hero, or as Pte. So-and-so, died of wounds ? It is deeds like this which make the Honours Lists so tragic. Sergt. X. has won the D.C.M. for some act of conspicuous bravery. You read further, and hear what the deed was. He has earned the medal. Always. But what about the other men who have done exactly the same act ? What of the man whom you yourself saw doing it the moment before he fell ? For one the D.C.M. For the other " Missing, believed killed." It does seem hard.

Have I been altogether too gloomy ? I'm sorry. And I don't want you to get the idea that things are often as bad as they have been during the last week, because they are not. Barring a certain amount of unpleasantness the life is not so bad, but owing to several things, chief of which was the succession of snow and rain, following upon the pulverising bombardment, the conditions just on this one part of the

line just for those few days were, in the words of a
man who has been out since the start, " worse than
anything they ever dreamed of in the first winter."
One thing though, and that is that the Germans have
been suffering far worse than we. All the time we
were there we were hardly shelled at all, but our guns
were going hard. We've got the shells, and we know
we are winning now.

Your
THOMAS.

THE GARDEN,

March 23rd.

PHYLLIS MINE,
    Back in the trenches of former days, but not
in the château any longer. It still stands there quite
untouched, but one day something is sure to happen
to it. 'Cos why ? 'Cos a Hun plane was brought down
the other day and on it was found a map. On the
map was found our ancestral home, marked as a headquarters, and in each corner of the garden the Huns
had got a 9.2 marked down. They weren't far wrong
either, and so we 'opped it pretty quick. Go along
the main road to Ypres and sooner or later you will
come to a garden. I can remember it about this
time last year when it contained a crop of cabbages.
Now it contains a crop of dug-outs—and Us. By
rights it should be a fruit garden, but I wouldn't give

much for this year's crop of peaches, and it was with something very much like a plum-tree that the fire was made this morning.

So here we sit and carry on the war, and if it isn't quite as comfy as the shatoo it's ever so much safer.

The death of a pig has been the cause of some rather amusing correspondence. Here it is as far as I can remember it.

I. From Claims Officer —th Corps to —th Corps.— " I beg to report that M. Pierre Gaston, of X., claims that one of his pigs was poisoned by the troops billeted in his farm during the month of February. He claims 1000 francs for the loss of the same."

II. From —th Corps to —th Division.—" For your report on demise of pig."

III. From —th Division to —th Brigade.—" This occurred in your billeting area. Report should therefore be furnished as to exact circumstances under which this unfortunate animal met with its fate, and disciplinary measures taken to prevent a recurrence of the incident."

IV. From —th Brigade to —th Battalion ; —shire Regiment.—" Can you report as above, or throw any light upon this lamentable matter ? "

V. From —th Battalion to —th Brigade.—" With reference to above. Enquiries have been made, but it has been found impossible to obtain exact particulars of the last moments of this poor creature. It is, however, thought that, unable to satisfy its hunger on the frugal fare supplied it by the thrifty farmer, the deceased must have approached the refuse pit of Number 12 platoon and appeased its gnawing pains upon the contents thereof. It was found in that vicinity on the morning of the 17th ult. in a nechrose condition. The fact that the aforesaid refuse pit was liberally sprinkled with creosol is thought to have been the cause of the loss of life of the unhappy quadruped. No estimate of the value of same can be given, as the party which assisted at the interment consisted of an ex-bricklayer, an ex-postman, an ex-draper, and an ex-drunkard. If the animal was the same as that which entered the room of the adjutant it is thought that it cannot have been worth 1000 francs, as even then, when still alive, it seemed to be in an advanced state of decay. The body can, however, be exhumed and sent to corps headquarters if it is so desired, and if transport can be supplied for transmission. Under the circumstances it is submitted that although death was not due to natural causes it may be said to come under the ' Act of God ' class, and it is further submitted that this battalion shall not be held responsible for what was virtually a *fait de guerre.*"

VI. From —th Brigade to —th Division.—" Herewith report from Battalion Commander of unit concerned. It does not appear to have been the fault of his men that the beast became defunct, nor does it seem that disciplinary measures should be taken against anyone but the farmer, who does not seem to have educated his animals upon the latest hygienic lines."

And there the matter ends as far as we are concerned. And so must I, as it is time I went round the trenches.

Your
THOMAS.

P.S.—If anything happens in the next few days at the old spot don't you get worried, for, unlike the curate at the Mothers' Meeting, I shall not be there. Shall probably be taking a trip soon down to France to join the battalion, as an urgent chit came from the division saying I was needed at once. That shows you how much I am valued, doesn't it ? At least it would if they hadn't at the same time applied in exactly the same words for another hero who is in charge of the divisional dirt destructor !

2 a.m.,
March 27th.

This is a terrible war, darling, a terrible war. Away on the famous Mound at St. Éloi Fritz the sniper's rifle goes crack, crack. Back here in our little hut I sit writing to you. I wonder what wee Fritz is thinking about as he pulls the trigger. Probably his breakfast. He pictures to himself the frizzling sausage and the steaming mess tin of coffee which is going to make up for his cold and weary vigil. But I know what Fritz doesn't. He isn't going to have any breakfast. For as I write, down in the depths of the earth, in a filthy, smelly and altogether horrible little tunnel, two men are putting the finishing touches to a scheme which will give Fritz the sniper, and many of his comrades too, a helping hand on their way into the next world, that is if they have been good little Huns. If they have been bad ones it will start them in the wrong direction, but doubtless they will get there just the same.

For a week we have been working like niggers to get the show ready for the artistes who are going to perform. It hasn't been at all a soft job, as the amount of stuff to be carried up was enormous, and the Hun could spot us bringing up things and used to strafe accordingly. In addition to this the weather has been awful, continuous rain and pitchy black moonless nights. And now we are sitting here waiting until it is time to climb up to the old windmill and watch the fireworks. I was up at the place an hour and a half ago, and everything seemed so quiet, unnaturally quiet in fact, as the transport had all cleared off as fast as it could go. Nothing but the occasional crack of a bullet overhead gave away the secret that there was a war on, and in half an hour—oh, my hat !

Now I'm going to get on my things and go out and applaud.

The Afternoon.

It has been a great success. The mound is now seventy feet deep, and the prisoners have been passing the huts in little batches of thirty and forty, escorted by three or four divisional cavalry, fearfully pleased at riding along with their swords out.

The first batch that came along nearly died of fright. Not far from where we are there is the camp of a newly arrived battalion, none of whom had ever seen a Hun before in their lives. This battalion had been doing drill and had just been dismissed when round the corner came the bedraggled little cortège, two officers and a score or so of other ranks. Out of sheer curiosity the battalion bore down upon them to one man, armed to the teeth just as they had come off parade. The Huns broke and fled, despite the efforts of their guards to keep them in, and it was not for some time that they could be collected again. Seeing that ferocious horde bearing down upon them, they must have remembered the good old lie that the *Engländer* murder all their prisoners in cold blood. It was too much for them. There is not much difference between the batches of prisoners who pass. Generally there is an officer or two at their head, strutting along with his head very much in the air and looking for all the world like a sulky child who has been robbed of a coveted toy. Behind him come the humble cannon fodder, thanking their lucky stars that their appearance in that rôle is now at an end for the period of the war. The majority still seem dazed from the force of the explosions, but those who have recovered laugh and joke as they go by, sandbags wrapped round their heads in place of their caps, which have either been lost in the heat of battle (waiting with their hands stretched heavenwards) or " souveneered " by their captors. And in a day or two they will be back in Blighty. Oh, isn't it a terrible war ?

Your
THOMAS.

THE PRINCIPAL PUB IN POPERINGHE,
April Fool's Day.

P-h-e-w ! I've said farewell to the Salient, and to-morrow the first train to France is going to have me on board. Never have I been more thankful to leave a place, for during the last few days it has been keeping up its reputation for frightfulness to the full. We thought that we were going to be interested spectators, and nothing more, of the show, but after twenty-four hours we found ourselves featuring in the leading rôles.

As a spectacle it was marvellous, but as a place to live in the captured line was hardly desirable, even in war time. The papers say that we took three lines of trenches on a front of six hundred yards. They lie. We took the third line. The first and second had ceased to exist before the first of the attackers crawled over the parapet in search of immortality. The five mines which went up made the most unbelievable craters, the largest was over a hundred yards—yes, yards—across, and the smallest was about sixty. Between them they ate up the whole of the front line and the support trench, and in it a whole battalion. So that was all right, except for the battalion of *Jäger* of course. They must have had a messy end. We had three or four days of concentrated Hades up there, and were relieved last night, and now I am *en route* to join the battalion.

As I rode away this morning I felt, just for a moment, rather sad at saying good-bye to Ypres and the Salient. Up North the cathedral tower stood white in the sunshine, all that is left of it. Nearer to me the grey tower of Vlamertinge brought back memories of the second battle, memories of days and friends gone for ever. Away to the right little white puffs of shrapnel were bursting over dear dirty old Dickebusch. At a trot we clattered down the hill, and through the paved streets of Reninghelst. Before us stretched the road to Poperinghe. We broke into a canter, our old hairies buckling to eagerly. They, too, had had enough of war.

Remember little Belgium. Shall we ever be able to forget it ?

Cheero.

THOMAS.

"BON" TIMES

CHAPTER VIII

" BON " TIMES

THE QUARTERMASTER'S BILLET,
FRANCE,

April 6th.

DARLING PHIL,

Back to the army again. After long and weary wanderings I reached the battalion rest billets last night to find that they are up in the trenches. They have been there now for twenty-two days without relief, and during that time they have lost six men slightly wounded. This is the life for me. Isn't it funny, Phyllis, the way in which the people at home who haven't been out have one consuming desire—to come out and fight, whereas those who have been out for some time have only one idea, and that is to get into some cushy spot.

This is a topping little village, untouched by shell fire, and about five miles away from the front line. The front line, too, seems to be luxurious beyond belief, great dug-outs thirty feet underground and good communication trenches for miles. After the rickety sheds, protected by a single layer of bags, these dug-outs will seem veritable palaces, and to walk down a communication trench unseen and dry will be something of an experience.

Now I'm going to knock off and go to sleep, as I must make an early start to-morrow morning.

Your
THOMAS.

THE FRONT LINE ONCE MORE,

April 12th.

MY DEAR GIRL,

We are now in the front line, and, I don't want to frighten you more than I can help, but I am responsible for all that lies between you and about three hundred yards of German hate. In other words I find myself a company commander. Isn't it deplorable, Phyllis, that the British Army should ever come to such a sorry plight as this. Me a company commander. It is quite a good line in trenching too, and we make a speciality of deep dug-outs. The company headquarters (stand properly at attention there and don't grin) is most salubrious, thirty foot underground, and with two nice little bunks in it. In one corner stands what once was a most select white toilet table, whereat no doubt some French beauty communed with nature —and art. If it has any self-respect left it must have felt very ashamed at the Gold Flake tin which provided me with a wash, a shave, and a portion of a bath this morning. Water, except for the sort which grows in the bottom of a trench, is rather scarce, and has to be carried up in petrol tins. Consequently my man only allows me a tobacco tin full for my ablutions.

In addition to having a whole company to command I have one elderly gentleman to instruct. Doubtless he is far, far above me in the Army List, but he is at present seeing life under my wing. He is fifty or thereabouts, quite old enough to be my father anyhow, and is bald and a sportsman. Also he sleeps all day. And most of the night. When he isn't eating, or scratching.

The food is a bit of a come down after the luxurious life with the brigade. Yesterday my rations failed to put in an appearance, but nevertheless my servant produced an excellent breakfast of fried bread. After I had finished it I called him in and congratulated him on the success with which he had made a meal out of nothing. " Ah, sirrr," he exclaimed, " I thocht ye'd maybe like something a wee bit tasty for breakfast, sae I scrapit the grease off yon boots of yours and fried the bread in that." And I enjoyed it too.

For the first two days I was up here we were in support in quite the largest dug-out I have ever seen. At one end of it two companies lived in comfort, and at the other end were our quarters. And we used to think that a dug-out which held eight men was a large one. The only crab about it was the number of rats, but that seems to be the same all round here. The mice are a nuisance too, and if you like to send out a few traps you will earn my everlasting gratitude.

Must go my round now. Your

THOMAS

THE SUPPORT LINE,

April 20th.

DEAR OLD THING,

Though it mayn't sound very flattering, I am sitting down to write to you just to fill in the time. It is nearly midnight, and I am on duty. The company are, for the most part, out on fatigue, carrying rations, repairing the C.T.'s, strengthening the saps, and all the hundred and one little jobs which an all-seeing battalion headquarters provides for us in case Satan should find some mischief still for idle hands. I am left all alone, with nothing to do but to take an occasional stroll along the dark and dismal trench and check any tendency to somnolence in the sentries. It isn't very exciting, but nowadays I'm not out adventure hunting. These dark nights and these narrow precipitous stairs make you bless the gentleman who invented the tin hat. As you grope your way upstairs, or down for that matter, your head is continuously coming in contact with the beams of the staircase ceiling, and if it weren't for our pea-green atrocities there would be a good many smashed heads.

The day has been remarkable for the steady downpour of rain. When I say remarkable I am, of course, trying to be funny. After the war the foreigner who dares to suggest that Albion is the only country in which rain falls more than half the year will meet with scathing laughter. In fact the rate at which the water falls (not to be confounded with the water-rate which never falls but always rises) in this country is appalling, and the ephemeral consumption of glutinous France which adheres to each sodden British soldier (this has nothing to do with the rum ration) is almost as staggering to the average conception as it is to the feet of the humid individual as he ploughs, plods I mean, his weary way through the fetid ruins of a turnip field. Need I say that he is carrying on his person the unexpended portion of the day's ration. On his face there shines, diffuses I should say, a ruddy glow of good health, slightly soiled by the muddy drip from his shapely *chapeau*. And when I say shapely I mean shaped like a pudding basin. While he stands there with the muddy glow, I did say muddy glow, didn't I ? diffusing good health off his helmet in trickling streams, I'm sure I'm getting mixed somewhere, why isn't he getting on with the war ? Answer me that if you can. If you cannot, please state why you have not already done so and render a report complete with sketch map to this office before dawn, and issue to all men on three consecutive parades in the trenches or a tablespoon as the case may be.

With which she cast herself from him, her blue eyes shining like rubies. " Dear," he cried, " dear. . . ." " And likely to become dearer with food at the price it is," was her sweet reply as she peered at him through her sea-green eyes of brown. " I love you," he remarked casually, as he readjusted his gas helmet. ' And I love you too," she replied. " Love me if you will," he remonstrated, " but don't love me too. You ought to say twice." She stared at him remorselessly through the fair lashes of her scintillating mauve pupils. " And you call yourself a soldier," she purred. " No, I call myself early," was his response, " but I went to the model trenches at Earl's Court." " Earl's Court," she wailed, "and you my affianced husband."

I think I must have been wool gathering, judging from the previous paragraph or two. However, it has passed the time, and in another five minutes I can go off duty, if I can waken up the *ingénu* veteran. He's making enough noise for a major-general now. I can just see the top of his bald head peeping out from his blanket. A mouse has just run over his toes, but he's too fast asleep to mind. At this time of night the mice get very daring and hop about all over the place. They are a pest. By the way, too, they are not the only pest that hops in this dug-out, but perhaps it would be best to draw a veil over that side, one of the most terrible sides, I can assure you, of the horrors of war.

Good night.

Your slightly incoherent

THOMAS.

April 30th.

DARLING GIRL,

Your present of the mouse-traps synchronised (good word that) with our arrival at a mouse-infested dug-out. In five hours my servant caught twenty-five mice and two small rats with the six traps. They now form part of our equipment, and travel with us everywhere.

We are out of the trenches for a few days—we do eighteen in and six out now, but it's no hardship as they are such cushy trenches. Still, you do enjoy the few nights of pyjamas and the freedom from the ceaseless watch. We stay in a large house in the centre of the village, and sleep in one room, the six of us, and eat in another. The dining-room is decorated all round the walls with chalk drawings by a French soldier who was here before us. They are jolly good and very amusing, but some of them mightn't meet with the approval of the *Church Times*.

Badminton is our latest recreation, and we manage to get quite a number of games after parade hours. Out of the window I can see a game going on now. The machine-gun officer, who has a good reach, is playing with the transport officer, who has a true eye, against the quartermaster, a man with a strong wrist, who is partnered by the *padre*, who has a large stomach. Whoever plays with him has a hard job. We are also thinking of starting some cricket, as we have unearthed a bat and a ball from the tool chest of the armourer-sergeant.

Directly we get back from the trenches we rush to have a bath, and I can tell you we need it after eighteen days. The baths are in a disused water-mill, and are run by two light-duty men under the auspices of the brigade. You bathe in half an old beer barrel full of topping hot water. It is interesting to see how quickly the water changes colour too. The other day several of us were having a bath when along rushed an orderly with a gas alarm. We reached for our gas helmets, unrolled them and laid them down beside the baths, and then proceeded reluctantly to dress. Five minutes later we dashed out of the baths, a weird-looking crew attired in each other's tunics, kilts and boots, with ties, collars, and hose tops on anyhow. Of course it was a false alarm. They always are if you take any notice of them.

I'm just off to the dentist. He lives about seven miles away, and I've got to ride there and back on the company charger, which was chosen by my predecessor on account of its homely face and gentle gait. When it tries to trot it wobbles horribly at the knees, if horses have knees, but it is when it breaks into a canter that it excels itself. It throws itself several inches up into the air and comes down on exactly the same spot. On the whole I am inclined to believe that it moves fastest when it is walking. It can just about keep up with a column on the march then. I'd use spurs but I don't think it would be any use. Not that I care for spurs in the ordinary way. They are so dangerous. If you are walking you are apt to trip over them, and if you are riding there is always the danger that they will touch your horse. Still I suppose they look nice.

Cheero.

Your
THOMAS.

P.S.—Wish I hadn't to go to the dentist. It is the first time I have ever been to an army one. I expect he will pull my teeth out by numbers.

THE COAL CELLAR,
VILLAGE INN,
E . . . . E,
May 10th.

PHYLLIS MINE,

We are staying at the principal *estaminet* in the place. The first floor has entirely disappeared, and so has the ground floor, except for a portion of the bar. So we inhabit the coal cellar. It is about ten feet broad and fifteen long, and has a coal-smeared arched roof strengthened by wooden struts in case it gets crumped. Along either side there runs a brick ledge, and along the brick ledge there run—well perhaps we needn't go into that too closely. These ledges we have covered with sandbags and they make fairly comfortable beds at night and seats by day. You descend to this haven of rest down a flight of slippery stone stairs,

but, though it is so far down, the morning sun manages
to find its way in, when there is any sun.   Our furniture
consists of one old oak table (a genuine antique), a
shake-down bed made of biscuit boxes and x-pip-emma,
or expanded metal to be more exact, and that is all.
Oh, and there is a telephone, but that is out of order,
thank the Lord!   Back here a " dissed " telephone
wire is a blessing in disguise.   " The R.E. want a
fatigue party of fifty men to help them with the new
C.T.," says the adjutant.   " All right," says the C.O.,
" detail them from B Company."   The adjutant goes
off to the 'phone and comes back with the news that
B Company's line is " dissed."   One of the other companies gets the job and we slumber on peacefully.

This must have been a pretty little place at one time,
but it has gone the way of all villages which grow a
few hundred yards behind the trenches and are used
as strong points.   However, there are still some
gardens in more or less good condition, and at any
time we like during the day we can wander out unseen
and pick daffodils in the grounds of the ex-château.
But it is at dusk, when the German lines are gradually
fading away into the evening shadows, that I like to
get out and wander through the *padre's* garden, which
by day is in full sight of the Hun.   Along deserted
gravel paths, now sprouting with new green grass,
borders of the most beautiful white narcissus on either
side, through sheltered walks fragrant with violets,
into the fruit garden, a mass of pink and white blossom.
There I love to stay and watch the setting of the sun

and the first gleaming white lights shot up by the anxious sentries at the foot of the hill. And when I begin to feel too sentimental I pull myself together and loot a bunch of spinach and the best of the rhubarb for our dinner. The spring onions are nearly ready, and the asparagus won't be long now. It is rather a find for me, as when an orderly comes along from Battalion H.Q. with a bit of a stinker in the way of chits, please explain delay and all that sort of thing you know, I send him back with a soothing answer and a prime cauliflower. They are beginning to count on me for their supply of " vegs."

We had a bit of a scare the first night up here. Just as we were going off to sleep a terrible racket started, and my servant fell downstairs in his eagerness to tell me that a mine had gone up some way to our left. Our job here is to check the victorious Hun, flushed with success at having broken through our trenches, and to drive him back to his spiritual home like melting snow on a summer's morn. Like antelopes we sprang to our posts, shivering with—no, not fear—cold. Around us the shells burst in myriads, one was not three hundred yards away, but undaunted we stuck to our posts, holding the fort, and throwing suitable portions of the chalky substratum at the rats whom we could hear nibbling away at our barbed wire defences. Heroes all. Us, not the rats. At four o'clock everything was quiet again, and we went off to bed. We never heard what it was that had happened, but it was probably a very minor affair.

I must stop now as I have important work to do.

Your

THOMAS.

P.S.—Last time I had the same important work to do I forgot to take the cards with me to the bombing officer's place, and had to come back and get them.

THE FRONT LINE,

May 22nd.

DEAR,

I'm feeling about as courageous as a jelly-fish. In this sector of the line there are some mine galleries, and the Hun knows it full well. And as Fritz has a rooted aversion to taking a toss at the hands of a mine, he is at great pains to prevent any unseemly underground disturbance of that nature. His aversion has taken the concrete form of a giant trench mortar which fires enormous aerial torpedoes at us from eleven hundred yards away, despite the attentions of our artillery to its supposed lair. And of all the damnable inventions of this war the trench mortar, especially the grown-up sort, is the most damnable. I have seen men so shattered by the concussion of one of these blighters that all they could do was to sit down and weep by the hour, and I saw some German prisoners, taken on the occasion on which we first used our new machine, who were worse still. They were clean dotty. Well this big chap has been going strong at the mine

galleries ever since we came up into the front line for
this trip, and as company headquarters is situated
plumb in the middle of the galleries we are having no
end of a time. If they start strafing a bit of trench it
isn't so bad. You can always move away to one side,
but company headquarters is the first link in the
chain which connects the bomber in the advanced
sap with the General Staff at the War Office, or the
Daily Mail, or whoever it is that is really running the
war. And so you must have some one there. To-day
we should have had to stay whether we liked it or not,
as the first three bombs smashed the trenches to bits
on either side of us and blocked up the C.T. to the rear.
To get away from the dug-out we should have had to
climb right over the blockage, and that would have
been " finee " for us. So there we sat for several hours,
while the dug-out shook from side to side. Occasionally
a more than usually near explosion would fill the whole
room with choking dust and smoke, but for the most
part they did nothing but make the dug-out rock to
and fro. The breathless waiting for the next one to
come is the most horrible part of it. To your straining
ears there comes a faint pop, and you know that it
has started. You do not actually hear the bomb until
it is on its downward course. Then you can just make
out a faint sssssssh, like the wind whistling among the
trees. It grows louder and louder, and then stops with
a plop as the bomb hits the ground. A fraction of a
second later comes the explosion, an indescribable
nerve-shattering explosion which tears down every-

thing within five yards of it and pulverises trenches, revetments, or anything which tries to withstand it. Oh, it's horrible. But as usual there is the light side, and to watch people hairing down the trench away from the falling terror is one of the most amusing things I know. All the more so if you happen to be one of them and you find yourself alive at the end. But what has made our nerves more fuzzy than anything else had nothing to do with the trench mortar. The strafing had ceased, and we were putting on our helmets with a view to going out and gathering up the fragments of our trench when there was a bang outside, and suddenly we were in the midst of a great hissing, roaring inferno. Everything seemed to be going round, and from the door came an overpowering red light and wave after wave of acrid smoke. " Bombs," cried my servant, who was in the act of laying the table. And here I regret to say that no one dashed to the rescue and flung himself upon the box of ignited hand grenades. No one was out for the V.C. And besides it wasn't bombs at all, but our rockets. A red-hot piece of shell must have swished downstairs and landed up in our box of S.O.S. rockets standing at the foot of the stairs. The show lasted for about five minutes, during which time the dug-out seemed to be full of flying, screeching red rockets and blazing green stars. We put our hands to our mouths to try and keep out the smoke, and resigned ourselves to fate. As it so happened nothing did hit us, for the box which held the rockets was on the lowest step of the stairs and

out of sight of the far corner of the dug-out. But only
by a few inches. People who were outside say that it
was a grand sight, long tongues of red flame and clouds
of smoke issuing from the dug-out and visible for miles.
They seemed to think it was rather a joke. And so
may we. After the war.

Sorry to have discoursed at such length upon my
own sufferings, but they are all over now, as we are
to be relieved at dusk.

Farewell.
Your
THOMAS.

P.S.—I have decided that it is more suitable for the
S.O.S. rockets to be kept in the signaller's dug-out.
In future they shall be.

BILLETS,

June 2nd.

DARLING GIRL,

One of the war's greatest lessons is that you
should not count your chickens before they're hatched.
I was going round the trenches with a certain officer,
who shall be nameless, and who has a reputation for
being rather "windy." He is my superior officer, by
a long way, and so, as becomes the perfect little company commander, I was escorting him round with
honeyed words, in the hope that he would remember
me favourably when next there was mention of a soft
job. We came to a nice secluded corner and my com-

panion sat down. So did I. He tilted up his tin hat
from his forehead and wiped the perspiration from his
brow. So did I, for it was hot, and he had been walking
fast, either in the laudable intention of seeing a lot,
or in the less laudable but more natural desire to get
back to his hole in the ground. " Phew," he remarked,
" it is hot." I assented. Silence. Then he broke out
again. " There's one thing I do like about these
trenches," said he, " you always know where the
Hun is going to drop his shells. What! Now this
place, for instance, the Hun has never shelled, and
never will if the war goes on for a hundred years.
What! What!" Before I had time to reply there
was a familiar swwwwish, and then whizz-bang, whizz-
bang, whizz-bang. We picked ourselves up from the
bottom of the trench where we had gravitated by some
natural instinct and grinned at each other. " What
a . . ." Whizz-bang, whizz-bang, whizz-bang. When
we were quite sure that the salvo was at an end we
hopped it in the most approved Derby winner fashion.
It was amusing, as the trench boards had been laid
down very badly, and every time the large foot of the
rapidly receding figure in front of me came down with
a flop on the nearest extremity of one, the other end
would jump up and hit him in the eye. That happened
three times, and each time he picked himself up I had
to pretend to stumble so that he should not see my
face. There was a large grin thereon. Poor chap, he
really is as brave as they make them, but he's a dug-
out and hasn't quite grasped the fact that this is an

ungentlemanly war. He judges things by the Crimea
or whatever the medieval scrap was in which he played
so dashing a part. In the army now there are three
classes of officers—the pre-war regulars, a first-class line
in soldiers but almost extinct among the infantry ; the
war-baby, the sort who weren't reared to be soldiers
you know ; and the hoary old dug-out, a patriotic
gentleman with gout and accustomed to use a blunder-
buss. And when you get Second-Lieutenant Dug-out
(Reserve of Officers) as one of Temporary Captain
War-Baby's subs there's hell to pay if both don't
possess a good deal of tact. Dug-Out, if he is a nice
old gentleman, will refrain from mentioning how they
would have done it in his time, how the they did it in fact
at the battle of Waterloo, Agincourt, or whatever it
was. War-Baby, on the other hand, will take care to
ask Dug-Out's advice on everything. With a little
wangling it ought to be easy enough to get him to say
the right thing on the majority of occasions, and on
the others you can always agree and then go and do
what you think best. War-Baby should also see that
he doesn't detail Dug-Out's platoon for any job in
which he is likely to get wet feet. It would also be
regarded as rather a touching sign of respect to his
senior in age if he tipped the wink to the company
mess orderly to serve Dug-Out first. If in addition to
this War-Baby can see his way to turning a blind eye
to Dug-Out's occasional absence from early morning
physical jerks, all will be well.

We are back for our six days in billets and are enjoying ourselves thoroughly. Last night we had rather a swell dinner, with two guests, in our company mess, but it was slightly marred by a misunderstanding on the part of the mess orderly. We started off with sardines as an *hors d'œuvre*, with kidney soup (tinned variety) to follow. With the roast beef was brought in champagne, or the stuff what masquerades under that name in this part of the country, and after that fruit salad and custard. Then the orderly came with the savoury. It was to have been a kippery sort of mess on a bit of toast, but some one had blundered, and he brought us each an enormous fish on a wee square of toast. We shrieked with laughter and swallowed the insult.

Talking about dinner, two swallows have started to build a nest over the fire-place in the messroom, and they carry on quite unperturbed by the other occupants. They fly in and out of the window, and if that is shut they bang their wings against the glass until some one lets them in or out. Our latest sub, who has to sleep in the messroom, feels rather bitter about this, as they keep flitting about all night long and they insist on using the window directly above him, and so he has the choice of getting out of bed to attend to their wants or of having the window wide open and getting soaked every time it rains. There is a telephone wire stretched across the room from the door to the window and the two sit on this while we feed, and look down at us with faint interest. "How sweet," I can hear your old charwoman saying as she picks up this letter while you are out of the room and reads this touching incident of a grim war.

Now I think I have babbled sufficiently, so good night.

Your

THOMAS.

BACK TO SCHOOL AGAIN

CHAPTER IX

BACK TO SCHOOL AGAIN

—TH ARMY INFANTRY SCHOOL,

June 11th.

DEAR OLD THING,

This is a startling change in my address, isn't it ? but it's all for the best I can assure you. About a week ago the M.O. came up to me. " Is there anything you'd like better than a month's rest ? " said he. " Why, yes," I replied, " two would suit me better." " What do you say to a month's advanced infantry course ? " " I'm on, but I don't know how to form fours." " That's all right. The C.O. said that I better let him know who's most in need of a rest, as he has to detail some one to go to this course." And so here am I, but, Lord, Phyllis, they do get rattled if you suggest to them down here that you are having a rest. They seem to think that it is hard work to drill and mess about from nine to five, but I'd drill for longer than that if at the end of it I knew there was a good dinner and a nice bed with white sheets awaiting me, as there is in this case.

We are a funny collection, one captain from each

battalion in this army. Old captains, young captains, fat captains, thin captains, captains in fact of all sorts, shapes, and sizes. Some of them are regulars, some Territorials, and some Kitchener's Army. Some have rows of ribbons, others have very new-looking braid on their sleeves. But to whatever species we may belong makes no difference. We are divided up into squads of about twenty, and carry rifles and have to look as military as possible, which of course is hard on some of us.

There was great indignation on the first day when it was seen that we had to rise up the next morning at six-thirty to do simple rifle exercises. Wasn't this to be an advanced course, and besides hadn't we been teaching men to slope arms for years and years, not so many years perhaps for some of us, and to suggest that we couldn't do it ourselves was a downright insult. But when the morning came and we fingered the great clumsy things, which belonged by rights to our servants, there were a few of us who began to doubt our capabilities, and when the dread word was given, " Slope arms," our actions would have shamed the rawest bunch of recruits alive. From Captain Oldboys, who did it like this in the Militia fifteen years ago, to Captain Wheeler of the Divisional Cyclists, who had never done it at all, nearly everybody was hopelessly wrong, and it was a very chastened gathering which slunk into the messroom for breakfast.

Altogether we are having a topping time, and are relearning a lot which has leaked out of our minds during the weary months of trench warfare. The whole thing is rich in humorous incidents, in fact they are so numerous that I can never stop laughing when I am supposed to be standing rigidly at attention. To look down the line and see the reassuring abdomen of old K—— sticking out in front of the rest of the line, like a pronounced salient, is enough to send me into a fit of giggles of which the silliest schoolgirl would not be ashamed. It is just like being at school again except that you don't run the risk of being caned. In the afternoons we listen to lectures, at least all of us listen to some of the lecture, and some of us listen to all of the lecture, but some, I fear, overcome by the heat and a good lunch, fall asleep. This afternoon, for instance, the lecture was rather a dull one and the afternoon very warm. Gradually that after-dinner feeling, combined with the monotonous voice of the speaker, began to tell, and after half an hour hardly a soul was awake. Most unexpectedly the lecturer made a joke. One man heard it and laughed. The man next to him on either side woke up with a jerk and asked what it was all about. When he had whispered it to them they laughed, and woke up their immediate neighbours. At the end of five minutes the whole hall was awake and laughing. It was awfully funny to notice the way in which the laughter swelled as the story was spread round the awakening multitude. I had a good opportunity to hear it, for I was the one man sufficiently awake to hear it originally. I was sitting directly in front of the commandant. Perhaps that explains my wakefulness. Most of the lectures are very good though, and the speakers are all men who know what they are talking about. The only fault which they share is that each man considers his own subject to be the most important of the lot, but perhaps that isn't a fault after all. The result is amusing. Every lecturer finishes up in very much the same way. " There is one thing which will win the war, and that is "—and here the lecturer mentions the subject on which he is speaking, be it map reading or sanitation.

The country round here is simply topping. On all sides wooded hills and fertile plains, cornfields dotted with poppies, and vivid yellow patches of mustard. Down in the valley is the sleepy little town, and through it winds a sparkling trout stream. A day or two ago we had a bus ride through a great forest and came back in the moonlight. The object of our joy ride was to visit an old farm and to prepare a defence scheme. In these defence schemes we are quite little generals as we are allowed infantry by the thousand, not to mention guns and cavalry (all imaginary by the way). However, it is a very pleasant way of spending the time, and if it isn't a rest I never want one.

Am just off for the week-end to Tréport. This is a very advanced course.

Your
THOMAS.

THE INFANTRY SCHOOL,

June 23rd.

Still here, and having a great time.   We have just
returned from the attack of an enemy's position, a
line of white flags funnily enough, and are feeling a
bit limp, as it has been a sweltering day, and they
seemed to think that we ought to double about eagerly.
They don't seem to realise that we are here for the
rest.   It is a bit harsh.   I was in the supporting line
which merges with the firing line just before the final
charge.   After we had been going some time I found
myself lying next to a man whom I knew to have
started with the first line.   When I had recovered
breath from the short sharp rush I asked him what he
was doing.   " Can't you see I'm looking up into the
sky ? " said he.   He certainly was, his head on his
hands, in a position of ease.   I rather fancy that his
eyes were shut when I flopped down beside him.
" Well, I've been detailed to look out for hostile air-
craft," he explained, and this time his eyes really did
shut.   A little further on I came to still another man
apparently asleep, but this one was lying face to the
ground.   As I flopped down beside him he turned to
me.   " Sssh, I'm listening for sounds of enemy mining,"
and he shut his eyes and went on slee—listening for
sounds of enemy mining I mean.   I felt inclined to

join him, but just then I noticed a member of the instructional staff bearing down upon us, so I continued my advance. The final assault was a very ragged affair. I was a bit blown myself and thought that if when the moment came to charge I didn't double very fast it wouldn't matter very much. Unfortunately everybody else seemed to have had the same brain wave, and the impetuous charge started off as a jogtrot and ended up as a walk. Still, as my next door neighbour remarked when we were getting slanged for slacking, we took the trenches all right, so I don't see what all the trouble was about.

I'm feeling altogether too moist to go on writing, so au revoir.

THOMAS THE TIRED.

THE INFANTRY SCHOOL,

July 2nd.

This is the last Sunday of the course, and I'm feeling rather depressed to think that this month's holiday is so near its close. It has been great fun, and in a quiet sort of way we have learnt a good deal. I am writing this on the cricket field (*sic*) where we have been playing a match. I made ten, so you will see that my batting has improved a good deal since pre-war days. The first ball went for six in the direction of square leg. The second was a four over the wicket-keeper's head, a rare shot, and the third ball was correct in direction and elevation, so I thought it about time to take my pad off (we only go in for one these days of economising) and write you.

I bet you are all awfully excited about the Push. For days we could hear the rumbling of the guns, thirty miles away at least, and we all knew what was coming and more or less where it would be. But none of us knew when. Yesterday night came the news that it had started, and though we seem to have done well it doesn't look like a break through. Whenever there is a push people get too sanguine and think that we shall be in Brussels in a week and on the Rhine in two, but I very much doubt whether the object of this little show is really to break through. If we can kill and capture Huns galore and give them absolute Hades for several months it ought to give him a big shaking and at the same time give our army the experience which at least half of it hasn't got. Still, we shall see.

They manage to keep things a bit more quiet than they used to, though a certain amount did get out concerning the Push. The news would probably come up with the rations, the quartermaster having been told by the A.S.C. supply officer. Your post from home would contain one or two references to it. From the Casualty Clearing Station would come tales of extensive preparations to receive wounded. All these signs might be mere coincidences, but when you saw the cerise band on the hat of an elderly gentleman walking round the trenches you knew that the worst was in store. For the D.A.D.M.S., short for Deputy Assistant Director of Medical Services, is the stormy petrel of the Western Front. Whenever he appears in the front system there is trouble ahead. He comes into your dug-out and says a few well-chosen words on the sanitation, or lack thereof, in your trenches, but all the time his eye is roving round your abode deciding how many stretcher cases could be accommodated in it. And sure enough an hour or so after he has gone there comes along a chit from battalion H.Q. saying that your happy home is to be turned into an advanced aid post, and will you please clear out of it forthwith. Then it's a foregone conclusion, and you are quite prepared for the summons to meet the C.O. in his boudoir with all the other officers, and have a large document, labelled " secret and confidential " in blue pencil, read to you on the subject of your assaulting the German trenches, marked in red pencil, on a near date and at a time to be communicated later by special messenger. But this time, though everybody knew that it was coming, no one could say when or exactly where. The Huns seem to have had a rough idea, pretty rough in fact or they wouldn't have kept three battalions of the best selected Prussian Guards in the sector directly opposite us, one poor little Territorial battalion with no intentions whatever of attacking them.

I shan't write to you again until I am back with the

battalion, who, by the way, seem to have stuck fast in the same trenches. They haven't been out since I left them. Guess they are getting a bit dirty this dry and dusty weather.

So long.

THOMAS.

THE PUSH

CHAPTER X

THE PUSH

THE SAME OLD CUSHY TRENCHES,

July 11th.

Here I am, old girl, back to the grim relentless
struggle, but sorry to say that the battalion are
shortly going out to a rest, and probably the whole
division too. Now a rest is all very well, not that it
ever is a rest, but far-seeing veterans look ahead and
shake their heads. " Where are we going to after the
rest ? " they say significantly to one another. And
wherever we go we couldn't find a better spot than this.
But it is not to be, and at present we have portions of
another battalion in the trenches with us for instruction. They have been out from England exactly a
week and in two days they are to take over from us.
They will have to learn jolly hard for forty-eight hours.
I heard my servant carrying on the instruction of the
batman of the officer whom I am supposed to be teaching. He was a Cockney.

They had been talking for some time about various
matters, when the pupil asked :

" Wot abaht these 'ere French gals ? "

" Och awa' wi' ye. Whit wud I ken o' the lassies ? "

From my own private observations I should say he knew a good bit.

" If yer sees a peach standin' in the dore of a pub., and yer wants a beer, wot do yer say ? "

" I dinna ken hoo it wud be best f'r ye. Mind ye if it were me, I'd jest walk up tae her swingin' my kilt fine, and give her a wee——"

" Yes, but wot do yer say, I asked yer."

" If she were a bonny lassie I'd gie her a wee bit squeeze an' say, ' Mamselle bon poor ongly soldah,' an' if she says, ' Wee traybon,' ye've clicked. But if she says, ' Nahpoo,' you haven't. Then ye'd carry on, ' Je vooaim cherry donnee moi un baisin,' an' if it's dark eno' she'll gie ye a wee bit kiss."

" 'Ere I don't want no kisses from French gals, I wants beer, b double e r."

" Och, if it's jest beer ye're wantin' ye hold up a penny and say ' beer.' "

I'm afraid my servant led him astray, because, despite his vehement denial of any desire to kiss a French girl, I heard him repeating to himself as he laid the table, " Je vooaim cherry donnee moi un baisin." He evidently wasn't going to forget that.

Now I must go away and instruct my protégé how to build a block in a communication trench. I'm not sure that I know myself.

Cheero.

THOMAS.

A Little Town,
Far from the Guns,

July 19th.

Dear Girl,

March, march, march. For days we have been marching, marching, marching, and always farther away from the fighting, and now we have arrived at the spot where, according to rumour, we are to rest for a month and relearn the art of open warfare once again. Let's hope that rumour doesn't lie, for this is a most pleasant place, and the old lady on whom I am billeted thinks I am a colonel and treats me with the respect due to such an exalted rank, and has placed me in a really well-furnished room with a beautiful feather bed and all sorts of luxuries in the way of sheets and pillow-cases and nice white towels.

But we have had a job getting here. As you can imagine, our feet were about as soft as they could be after practically a whole month in the trenches, and with wet feet for the last week of that. The first day we only did ten miles, but it seemed like fifty, and every day since then we have been doing our fifteen or twenty, and curiously enough feeling fitter every day. One day we slept in a topping little village given over to the cult of the cherry. The old man of the house seemed to like us, and we lived entirely on luscious white-hearts in consequence. Our next halt was at a little place of a few hundred inhabitants, and

the accommodation was scarce. Poor old C——
dropped a brick here. The Q.M. showed him the house
at which he was billeted, and he approached it, thinking out the French for " Can I sleep here ? " The door
opened and revealed a buxom wench. In his polite
old-fashioned way C—— bowed. " Est-ce que je puis
me coucher avec vous ? " he enquired. I fear he will
bear the marks of that woman's finger-nails until his
dying day. That illustrates the old adage about the
danger of a little knowledge, doesn't it ?

I can't remember all the places at which we stopped,
but we have been going strong ever since the 13th,
six days of the intensest loathing for the man who
invented equipment. Now we seem to be settled
down for a rest, and the men need it. As for myself,
it seems to be nothing but rests now, doesn't it ? At
any rate I'm going to have a good old lie in bed to-
night, and nothing will get me up before 9 a.m. I'll
carry on with this to-morrow.

THOMAS.

July 20th.

I was going to lie in bed till nine o'clock, wasn't I ?
Well at nine o'clock I was thirty miles away from the
bed which I crawled into at eleven pip emma. I had
only just shut my eyes when a knock came at the
door, and an orderly entered. " Battalion to be
formed up ready to move by midnight, head of the
column opposite the market cross, D Company lead-

ing," and he had gone. Well, you know what's coming just as well as I did, and here we are in billets (billets mean the old German front line) and bang in the middle of the Big Push. We started to march just about midnight. The men of course had had no food since tea-time. At two-thirty we arrived at a station and waited in the cold for an hour or so till the train came. When everybody had been crammed in, eleven and twelve to each compartment, we started, and travelled till about ten. Then we fell out of the train and found ourselves standing beside a large wire cage, full of Huns. "Hullo, Jocks," cried one of them, "glad we're not you." We marched out of the station and along a dusty road. Coming in the opposite direction were bus loads of slightly wounded, as happy as men could be, singing and joking, laughing and talking, bound for Blighty. I'm afraid I envied them. After we had been marching for half an hour a halt was called, and the billeting party went on ahead. We lay down by the side of the road, spat the dust out of our mouths, and wondered how long they would be settling up our billets in the village just ahead. We formed up and moved on. No billeting party to meet us at the edge of the village. Or in the middle of it. Or at the further end of it. On we went, feeling absolutely done in. In front of us stretched a great dusty road, but no sign of our billeting party. An hour went by and we had a ten minutes' halt. Packs were thrown off and a large number of the men fell fast asleep. Then on again for another hour and another rest. Then on again. On

either side of us bivouacs were springing up, and soon
we were marching through an unending vista of wagon
lines, bivvies, and ammunition dumps. Strings of
horses, several hundred at a time, passed us on their
way to water, and a little band of weary prisoners
shuffled along, guarded by a single Argyll and Suther-
land Highlander. Suddenly we saw that longed-for
sight, our billeting party. Which side of the road was
our resting-place to be? Then came the disquieting
rumour that we had still five miles to go. The rumour
was true, and it was not till four in the afternoon that
we arrived at these trenches, our billets for a day or
two. And then?

I'm going to turn in now and get some sleep while
I can. There is a fifteen-inch gun within fifty yards
of us, and it makes a terrific row when it goes off,
but I shall be able to sleep through absolutely anything.

Good night.

Your footsore, dirty, but loving

THOMAS.

21st.

We are off into the thick of it this evening, up to
that ill-fated wood half a mile in front of the rest of our
line, so we shall see life with a vengeance.

Did I ever tell you about L—— who was at the
Infantry School with me? On the day that the Push
started he broke his ankle playing football against

the A.S.C. Now I hear that he arrived with the first
batch of Somme heroes at Charing Cross, and was
liberally strewn with roses, while he was pulling the
blanket all the more closely round him, so that nobody
should notice that he was still in footer clothes ! All
the way over, so he says, people seemed to make a
point of coming up and asking him where he had been
hit ! He must have felt a fool.

Cheero till I have time to write again.

Ever your
THOMAS.

A RED CROSS BARGE,
NEARING ABBEVILLE,

July 27th.

DARLING GIRL,

I have been too weak to write and tell you that
I'm all right, but my troubles are over now, I think,
and I'm feeling ever so much better.

The last few days have been rather sketchy ones as
far as I'm concerned. Endless journeys in bumping
ambulances (I always used to think an ambulance had
springs) some one standing over me and saying,
" Breathe in, breathe in," nurses asking me if I felt
better now, and above all incessant enquiries as to my
name, rank, regiment, age, service, and those two concluding grisly questions, religion and next of kin.
Otherwise nothing much.

Of those days up in the wood I can't write now.

They say I should get home in a few days. Till then good-bye. Isn't it a terrible war ?

Your
THOMAS.

What there is left of him.

APPENDIX
ILLUSTRATIONS

FLOWING WITH FAIR MAIDENS, FREE WINE

There's a Long Long Trail

AT THE REGULATION WALK OF ABOUT A MILE AND A HALF PER HOUR

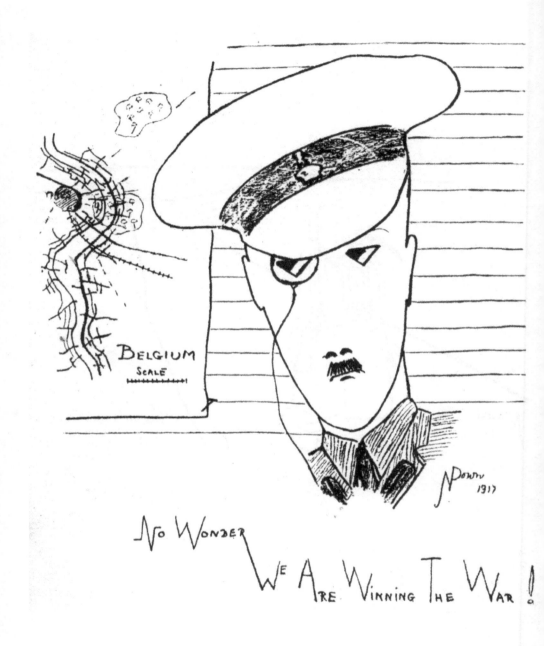

IT APPEARS THAT YOU WORK ON THE STAFF AFTER ALL

AS HEART-BROKEN AS AN A.S.C., M.T., OFFICER WITHOUT SPURS

NOT MUCH GLORY ABOUT IT

PERCHED WELL ON THE SIDE OF MY HEAD

NOT MUCH GLORY ABOUT IT